'An entertaining and informative book. Anyone who is contemplating setting up a cellar in Australia should buy this book . . . the glossary at the back is invaluable.'

Vogue Entertaining

'Written in a very personal and anecdotal style, drawing on Halliday's immense knowledge and experience of wine. He goes back to basics in many parts . . . thereby answering the most-asked questions.'

Sydney Morning Herald

'James Halliday has distilled wisdom garnered over three decades to produce this book.'

Choice

'This is a practical book with straightforward information about the construction of the simplest to the most elaborate cellar . . . an extremely comprehensive guide for anyone ready to put down a dozen or more for later enjoyment.'

Wine & Spirit

'Well put together and a must for all wine buffs.'

The Standard, Warrnambool

'The seasoned wine collector will find it easy, entertaining reading. For the beginner it is an enthusiastic yet factual account of the efforts that go into and the pleasures that come out of a wine cellar.'

Canberra Times

james halliday

collecting
wine
you and your cellar

HarperCollins*Publishers*

HarperCollins_Publishers_

First published in Australia in 1989 by Angus&Robertson Publishers
Paperback edition published in 1992
This revised edition published in 1998
Reprinted in 1998, 1999 (twice)
by HarperCollins_Publishers_ Pty Limited
ACN 009 913 517
A member of the HarperCollins_Publishers_ (Australia) Pty Limited Group
http://www.harpercollins.com.au

Copyright © James Halliday 1998

HarperCollins_Publishers_
25 Ryde Road, Pymble, Sydney, NSW 2073, Australia
31 View Road, Glenfield, Auckland 10, New Zealand
77-85 Fulham Palace Road, London W6 8JB, United Kingdom
Hazelton Lanes, 55 Avenue Road, Suite 2900, Toronto, Ontario M5R 3L2
and 1995 Markham Road, Scarborough, Ontario M1B 5M8, Canada
10 East 53rd Street, New York NY 10022, USA

National Library of Australia Cataloguing-in-Publication data:

Halliday, James, 1938– .
Collecting wine, you and your cellar.
ISBN 0 7322 6528 2.
1. Wine and wine making – Australia. I. Title.
641.220994

Background photograph on cover by Oliver Strewe
Inset photograph on cover by George Seper
Set in Bembo 11/15pt
Printed in Australia by Griffin Press Pty Ltd on 79gsm Bulky paperback

9 8 7 6 5 4   99 00 01 02

about the author

James Halliday is Australia's most respected wine writer. Over the past 30 years he has worn many hats: lawyer, winemaker and grape grower, wine judge, wine consultant, journalist and author. He has now discarded his legal hat, but actively continues his other roles, incessantly travelling, researching and tasting wines in all the major wine-producing countries. He is currently Chairman of Judges at the National Wine Show, Canberra, the Royal Adelaide Wine Show and the Sydney International Wine Competition.

James Halliday has written or contributed to more than 30 books on wine and calculates he has also penned (he is still to master a computer) more than 1 550 000 words for his weekly wine columns (since 1983 for the *Weekend Australian*) and magazine articles. Various of his books have been translated into Japanese, French and German, and have been published in the United Kingdom and the United States as well as Australia.

His most recent works include *Classic Wines of Australia, An Introduction to Australian Wine,* a comprehensive guide to individual wineries and wines entitled *James Halliday's Australian and New Zealand Wine Companion* (1998 edition published as a book and CD-ROM), and a lavish new edition of the *Wine Atlas of Australia and New Zealand*, to be published for Christmas '98.

contents

Bass Phillip Pinot Noir
This is the rarest and arguably the greatest of the top-ranked Australian pinots, particularly the effectively unprocurable Reserve and Premium versions.

wine collecting

a communicable disease

I suppose I can blame my parents. One of my earliest memories is of their walk-in cellar, with its wrought-iron door, stone walls and wooden racks. The house, built around the turn of the century but remodelled in 1932, was on several levels, and the cellar was under the middle of the house but reached by the stairs which led to the lower level.

From the late 1920s it was stocked almost exclusively with Lindemans Private Bin wines, and in those days 'Private Bin' meant what it said, for nine out of ten bottles of wine drunk in Australia at that time were fortified: sherry and port ruled the day. Winemakers continued to make dry white and red table wines, but it was as much out of stubbornness (and for their own consumption) as anything else; they didn't really expect anyone to buy it.

What is more, Lindemans was then in the hands of a receiver, a state of affairs which was to continue until 1947. Even more remarkably, its principal offices and warehouse were situated in the basement of the Queen Victoria Building. It was here that, from 1930, my father was received with pomp and circumstance on his buying trips, and with near reverence as he sallied forth with half a dozen cases to go into the back seat of the car.

This, I hasten to add, started before my time. (I have 1938 as my birth year, a wretched year in Bordeaux but — praised be the Lord — a very good one in Burgundy.) So it was in the years immediately after the Second World War that I came to drink a small glass of wine diluted with an equal part of water whenever wine was served at the table.

With the passage of time, I became familiar with the Lindemans names — Hock, Riesling, Chablis, White Burgundy, Burgundy and Claret — and also with the vintages and the bin numbers (some of which, such as Bin 591 Hock, remain implanted in my memory). But none of us knew, or cared, that the white wines were made from a grape called semillon, the reds from a grape called hermitage. Even further from our ken was the knowledge that hermitage was called shiraz in South Australia. What was certain was that all wines made in the Barossa Valley tasted like jam.

For in those far-off days, wine was drunk with enjoyment but not introspection. It was sufficient to acknowledge at the first taste that it was 'jolly good' (and perhaps make a fleeting reference to an earlier vintage or a bottle of the same wine tasted six months or a year previously) before proceeding to the more important dinner-table discussion. Wine was there to serve, not to dominate; to be consumed, not to consume its idolators.

st paul's college: not only for study

But, as I say, the seeds were sown, even if it was to be some years before they germinated. The next phase was my six carefree years at St Paul's College, Sydney University, as I devoted a precisely judged amount of time to gaining an arts-law degree. One of the numerous pleasures of that time was the privilege of wine in the cathedral-like stone dining room on Wednesday night and at Sunday lunch. This in turn came (at cost) from the college wine cellar, and with it came the introduction to new and unfamiliar names.

Prominent among these were Penfolds and Tulloch, the latter supplied by the late Johnnie Walker and by Harry Brown of Rhinecastle Wines. Walker and Brown organised occasional trips to the Hunter Valley, and I made my first pilgrimage as a callow university student in 1957 or 1958 — I forget which. Johnnie Walker was the chef at the barbecue lunch provided at Tulloch, served on trestle tables resting on the earth floor between the ancient 500 gallon (2250 litre) casks in which the red wine was matured.

The trips multiplied; in those days Tulloch was one of the few family makers to bottle and label its whole output. Tyrrell's (which we also visited regularly) sold most of its wine in bulk, bottling in response to direct demand, and Drayton's and Elliott's did likewise. Cellar-door sales — at least as we understand that term today — did not exist, so my beloved Lindemans and McWilliam's (which completed the rollcall in those days) were infrequent courtesy calls.

At the end of 1961 I finished my law degree, and spent most of 1962 in Europe. A university friend and I bought a panel van and spent the summer of that year tracing our way from Spain to Norway. We drank wine copiously and unselfconsciously, choosing the cheapest *vin de pays,* which in Spain and Italy was extraordinarily (if not lethally) cheap. But we also drank the local beer, and at no time did our erratic path across Spain, France, Italy and Germany turn on the presence or absence of vineyards and wine. My major discovery, indeed, was that the raffia-covered chianti flask of Italy came in two sizes, 750 millilitres and 1.5 litres. A single-sitting demolition of the latter size (believing it to be no more than a standard bottle) highlighted our first night on the outskirts of Rome.

I returned to Australia late in 1962 to confront the grim reality of earning a living and making a career. My ties with Lindemans continued, and I became the wine-buyer for the house I shared with two of my workmates at my law firm. The savings engendered by being able to buy direct were more than counterbalanced by the rate of consumption: our 'house' wine of the time was Lindemans 1962 Bin 1930 Riesling, which was delivered in four- and five-case lots, and consumed almost immediately. A few bottles remain in my cellar to this day, unlikely survivors of an era.

my first cellars: under my bed, then in the linen cupboard

The range of wine broadened in the aftermath of an Easter foray to Rutherglen by one of my housemates; vast quantities of 1954 and 1958 Baileys red followed him back to Sydney to be triumphantly collected one Saturday morning at Darling Harbour goods yard. The cost was five shillings and sixpence (55¢) a bottle, and it was particularly successful at barbecues. During this period I established a cellar of sorts underneath my bed, security being one of the major considerations.

There was room under the house, but it proved a vulnerable storage place during parties, particularly if one happened to be absent from the house at the time.

I moved out in 1966 to become caretaker of my parents' house while they took an extended overseas trip. My embryonic cellar was then moved from under the bed to the far grander surroundings of the formal stone cellar, and the collecting disease started to take hold. On their return, I moved into a new apartment building in Paddington, which was complete with spacious built-in linen cupboards. The shelves of the floor-to-ceiling cupboard quickly became my next cellar; I was inordinately proud of the 300 or so bottles which I had accumulated, and delighted in dramatically flinging open the door to show my guests.

the wine odysseys become serious

Very rapidly, however, the overflow situation became critical, and I started to store unopened cases under friends' and relatives' houses. My parents had by this time retired to Moss Vale, and in no time cases had started to accumulate there as well. The cellar received a considerable boost in 1968 when, together with my former housemates, I embarked on my first wine odyssey. The correspondence file on the trip is a testimonial to the hospitality which has always been extended by the wine industry: we were completely unknown to most wineries, and simply wrote 'cold', giving our itinerary and indicating that we hoped we would be able to visit. The replies were unfailingly courteous. What is more, many were signed by winemakers who have since become firm friends (but who I am perfectly certain would be most surprised to be shown their letters).

We left Sydney on 16 March and drove to the Barossa Valley via Mildura (and Mildara), where on 18 March an invoice records the purchase of one dozen 1963 Mildara Coonawarra Cabernet Sauvignon at $24.60 per dozen. 'Peppermint Patty', as the wine is now nicknamed, sells for up to $300 per bottle at auction these days.

A box trailer was hired in Adelaide, and after spending a week in the Barossa Valley, Clare Valley and Southern Vales we returned to Sydney via Coonawarra, Great Western, Tahbilk and north-east Victoria. Even by the time we left South Australia the trailer was dangerously overloaded, and all subsequent purchases (of which there were numerous) followed us back to Sydney either by truck or rail. A letter from Brown Brothers indicates that there was a problem with the freight charges: Ross Brown apologetically explained that the basic freight rate of 28¢ per carton applied only on a Brown Brothers-to-freight depot delivery and the door-to-door delivery had resulted in a 70¢ charge.

a proper cellar at last

By the time I married and built my first house in 1969, I had wine stored in five different locations stretching from Sydney to Moss Vale. The house was a split-level Habitat, a merchant builder's house which was, however, substantially modified. One of the modifications was the provision of a concrete slab for the floor of the dining room, kitchen and laundry. This became the roof of the cellar, reached by an internal door on the lowest of the three levels of the house. The builders were instructed to specially excavate underneath the concrete slab for half of the length of the house, and this was to be the cellar. Inadvertently, however, they excavated the entire length, and I ended up with a cellar that was far larger than I had planned. It seemed only sensible to take advantage of the builder's mistake, and to concrete the floor the entire length.

About this time, the New South Wales Bottling Company was selling old galvanised-iron beer crates for $1 each. Several Avis truck trips later I had the 400 crates safely home, and for the first time in my life had the luxury of an accessible cellar.

My happiness knew no bounds; each rack was labelled with Dymo tape, and I knew precisely where every one of the 3000 or so bottles I had accumulated was. But I also had space to spare: more beer crates followed, as did wine to fill them. It was at this time that I first became seriously interested in the wines of France, and began buying at Christie's auctions in London. Periodically, shipments would arrive providing another influx of wine to deal with. Racks overflowed, wooden boxes sat in the centre of the floor, and the 3000 bottles became 6000.

the pain of moving house — and cellar

Ten years after it was built, the house was sold. Like a hermit crab with an outsized shell, I painfully moved the cellar to temporary storage under the house of the well-known Sydney retailer, Andrew Simon of Camperdown Cellars. After a year or so of peripatetic flat dwelling, I took space in a Pyrmont warehouse, and once again commenced the slow business of establishing an orderly cellar.

The number of bottles had continued to grow, by now exceeding 10 000, so substantial additional racking was necessary. With the help of friends, I erected steel reinforcing mesh in two vertical panels, braced with tubular galvanised iron and crosspieces. These were set against the wall; the wire beer crates were stacked back to back in rows along the middle of the cellar.

It took a very long time to organise and re-catalogue the cellar; access to the warehouse was difficult, as it was protected by numerous burglar alarms which as often as not I succeeded in setting off when entering out of hours. But I persisted, and by the time 1983 arrived all was orderly.

In the middle of that year fate took an unexpected turn and I moved to Melbourne to help build up the newly established Melbourne branch of my law firm. There was an ulterior motive: in 1980 I had identified the Yarra Valley as the place to which I wished ultimately to retire, to grow grapes and make wine. But at that time I was still heavily involved in the Hunter Valley vineyard and winery which, together with Tony Albert and John Beeston, I had founded, and the Yarra Valley seemed distant both in terms of time and place.

But the break-up of my first marriage, the opportunity of helping build a new law office, and of course the enticement of the Yarra Valley made the decision far easier than it might otherwise have been. So I set off to Melbourne with my present wife Suzanne, and leased a lovely two-storey Victorian terrace house in Millswyn Street, South Yarra. Not trusting transport companies and lacking the courage to obtain a quotation for the removal of the cellar, we made four trips from Sydney to Melbourne in a variety of hired trucks and trailers, including a horse float.

moving again: from pain to agony

It rapidly became apparent that the time (and the cost) of moving the cellar this way was out of the question. After some discussion and negotiation, Grace Brothers took on the job. In the meantime, warehouse space had been acquired at Flemington, and ARC racks (of the type I describe in Appendix 7) had been installed in readiness. It was now summer, and it was agreed that the wine (which had been removed from the Pyrmont racks and packed into removalist boxes, every bottle wrapped in bubble plastic, and with a conventional wine box inside the removalist's box) would be packed into two rail containers and shipped to Melbourne overnight.

On the appointed day the railways went on strike. The containers, weighing 25 tonnes in all, were put on semitrailers and moved by road. When unloaded at the Melbourne end they filled the rented warehouse area to the point where there was just enough room to inch one's way along each side between the racks and the boxes.

Grace Brothers had done an absolutely magnificent job, breaking not a single bottle, but my joy was short-lived. On unpacking the first box, I found 12 different bottles of wine; the second was the same; so was the third, the fourth and the fifth ... The light dawned: in Sydney the wines were arranged in the racks vertically, with 22 bottles in each vertical line. Instead of noticing the capsules or the labels, and following the racks up and down, the Grace Brothers staff had packed by picking across the racks. To compound the matter, there was no index of boxes. What should have been a relatively simple task of unpacking became a nightmare, an endless process of sorting, moving, resorting and removing.

I consoled myself with the thought that I had no intention of moving house for at least five years, and that the arrangement was at least reasonably long term, and that — when the arduous task was finished — I would once again have an orderly cellar. I was also enormously helped by my wife Suzanne, who not only unloaded the original containers, but who did a great deal of the unpacking and preliminary sorting. It took 12 months to finally organise the cellar, which by this time amounted to well over 16 000 bottles. A short period of cellar-calm followed, but in mid-1985 a property came on the market in the

Yarra Valley which we decided we simply had to buy, money or no money. The purchase price successfully borrowed, the property was purchased, and early in 1986 we moved in.

never again: only an earthquake

One of the great attributes of the 12-year-old house was its hillside position, with panoramic 250-degree views of the Yarra Valley spread out below it. It also sat on a cantilevered concrete slab built into and projecting from the hillside. Underneath, the entire slab was repeated, creating a vast open undercover parking area. It was the simplest of matters to fill in between the supporting columns of that area with a double brick wall, adding insulation between the two lines of bricks.

The result was the best cellar one could possibly have, unless it be totally underground. But of course the wine was in Melbourne, over 50 kilometres away, with the last five kilometres being dirt road, and the last half kilometre a narrow, climbing, twisting access road which only small trucks can pass.

Suzanne took the interminable repacking and trailer trips from town in good spirit. A few thousand bottles of surplus wine went off to auction to ease the move, and towards the tail end a friend of a friend provided a bread delivery van in off-hours at modest cost, and the move was finally completed. So once again I am united with my cellar. A landslide may move it. Nothing else will.

The most common reaction of visitors seeing the cellar for the first time is to exclaim 'But how on earth are you going to drink it all?' The answer is simple: I have not the least intention or expectation of drinking it all. I am more than happy to leave that task to those of my relatives and friends who survive me. I also happen to regard it as a near-certain guarantee of long life. It has often been said (although I believe incorrectly) that when the great wine expert and wine-lover André Simon died in his eighties, he had only one bottle of wine left in his cellar. Those who tell this story then go on to say, 'How wonderful, what perfect timing.' I prefer to say that it was precisely *because* André Simon had only one bottle of wine left in his cellar that he died. Clearly, one could never drink one's last bottle, so there was nothing left to live for. While I am sure that my children and friends will possess fine palates by the time my allotted span is over, a considerable number of the bottles waiting to be drunk are those which I could trust only myself (in the company of friends, of course) to properly evaluate and appreciate.

Which leads to the last observation: having got over the shock of the size of the cellar, people's next reaction is to point to a particularly old or rare bottle and say, 'How could you ever bear to drink that?' Once again, the answer is simple: how could I bear not to drink it? Wine is not like a postage stamp, frozen in a time warp on the page of an album. It is there to be drunk; the older, the rarer, the more exquisite, the more it demands to be drunk. There is no greater pleasure than sharing such a bottle with one's friends.

PETALUMA

1995 RIESLING

750ml

PRODUCE OF AUSTRALIA BOTTLED AT PICCADILLY SA

Petaluma Riesling
The grape variety, the Clare Valley and the skills of
Brian Croser combine to make Australia's foremost
riesling which progressively unfolds in bottle for
over a decade.

wine

a living thing

the fascination of wine can be attributed to one basic characteristic or property: it is a 'living' thing which continues to change from the moment it is made to the moment it is at last consumed.

From this simple property stems the fact that no two bottles of wine are precisely the same, even though in young wines bottled under sterile conditions in an inert atmosphere the difference may not be measurable by scientific analysis or detectable by the most sensitive palate.

But as the years go by, those two bottles which came off the same bottling line (and which are stored next to each other in identical conditions) will gradually assume different characteristics. It is true that to a lesser or greater degree these differences may ultimately turn upon differential rates in the chemical ageing of polymers — and less commonly on bacterial activity — but there will have been an earlier stage before these processes became established, when an all-seeing eye, an all-encompassing palate, would already have been able to detect and describe differences in the two bottles had the corks been drawn.

The differences will in the ordinary course of events be attributable in part to the corks placed in the bottles — for no two corks are precisely the same. Air, or oxygen, passes slowly along the sides of the neck beside the cork; the passage may be infinitesimal, or it may be much larger (though still not visible to the naked eye, of course). This will be determined principally by the quality of the cork (there are three grades generally recognised in the cork trade), but also by the configuration of the bottle neck.

corks, bottle necks and ullage

For reasons which I do not fully understand, Australian bottle makers find it technically difficult to make a bottle with a completely even neck. Push your little finger inside the neck of most bottles and you will feel a distinct bump or ridge halfway down the neck. This causes the cork to distort or stress as it is inserted in the bottle, and may cause a less perfect seal than would otherwise be obtained. It is as much for this reason as any other that the ullage (the airspace between the bottom of the cork and the top of the wine) in a 20-year-old Australian red wine will typically be far greater than that in a comparably aged French red wine.

The figure on page 87 shows the ullage level accepted as normal in French wines of varying ages, assuming the wines have not been topped up and recorked at any stage of their life. This recorking is a relatively common practice at the great chateaux of Bordeaux for their reserve or museum stocks. Chateau Lafite, indeed, sends one of its head cellarmen on periodic worldwide trips to 'officially' recork old bottles of Chateau Lafite held in private cellars. (I describe the topping-up and recorking process in greater detail in Chapter 8, for it is a practice to be encouraged.)

the penfolds red wine clinics

In the early 1990s Penfolds began its Red Wine Clinics, conducted in conjunction with Langton's Fine Wine Auctions. A highly sophisticated mobile corking machine, equipped with vacuum jaws, tours major Australian cities. Owners of Penfolds Grange, St Henri, special show bins (60A, 80A, Bin 7 etc.) or old and rare Penfolds reds can register for the clinics (via **freecall** 1800 025 531) and have ullaged bottles inspected and, if appropriate, opened.

A small sample of the wine is removed and tasted by the senior Penfolds winemakers, headed by John Duval. If the wine is still in good condition for its age, it will be topped up with wine of similar type, recorked, and given a special back label specifying the recorking date and certified by Langton's. If it is unsound, the bottle will simply be recorked, and the owner advised to drink it — or cook with it.

The ullage is normally created very slowly; a little oxygen makes its way into the bottle as the wine cools and contracts during winter months.

As the wine warms up in summer, the volume of wine expands and a little wine is expelled along the sides of the cork. Depending on the rate of discharge, it may evaporate immediately on contact with the air, leaving little or no visible sign on the cork. In a temperature controlled cellar this process of interchange will be slowed enormously; in a cellar with a diurnal temperature range of 10 degrees Celsius (a fluctuation from 15 to 25 degrees Celsius is not uncommon in Australia) the process will speed to a gallop.

The ullage level is the first guide to indicate the likely condition of an old bottle of wine. (In this context I use 'old' to mean a wine that is more than 20 years old, and 'very old' to denote wines that were made more than 50 years ago.) If the ullage level is lower than the typical ullages shown in the figure on page 87, then there is a probability (but not a certainty) that the wine will demonstrate excessive deterioration and may well either be badly oxidised or show marked acetic volatility. Both of these probabilities increase with age, although paradoxically so do the exceptions. In other words, an abnormally ullaged young wine will invariably show gross deterioration, but an old wine that is similarly ullaged may actually be superb. Ullage change is likely (though not necessarily) to be less damaging if it occurs over a long period of time.

the colour changes of age

The second quality guide in old wine is its colour. If the bottle glass is dark, it takes a trained eye to evaluate the depth and the hue, but it can be done. In the case of white wines, the lighter the colour, the greater the promise. With red wines, the position is precisely reversed: the darker the better. The emphasis is on the word *guide*: this is not an infallible yardstick. I well remember opening a bottle of 1959 Kreuznacher Brückes Trockenbeerenauslese a decade ago. The colour in the glass was that of a very old muscat, dark brown with an olive-green rim. My heart sank: I was at a BYO restaurant, and the wine was intended as a crowning piece to the meal, which had seen a remarkable range of wines including a 1923 Chassagne-Montrachet, a 1926 Beaune and an 1877 Chateau Pomys, all of which had opened superbly. I need not have worried: the wine had retained every bit of the intensity and searing lusciousness which had made it one of the most celebrated of all Trockenbeerenauslesen.

Clarity may or may not be a guide. Much depends on the care with which the wine has been handled in the days and hours prior to its inspection. If it has lain undisturbed in the cellar and is carefully removed (still on its side) for examination, it should be crystal bright. If it is even a little cloudy or dull, there are problems which may stem from bacterial activity. This is not a common occurrence, however; the more usual situation will be a deposit in the bottle, which may be fine (and therefore easily disturbed), coarse and crystalline (not easily disturbed), or caked on to the side of the bottle (disturbed only by vigorous movement).

deposits, sediments and wine diamonds

Contrary to commonly held opinion, such deposits are not in themselves inimical to quality. But for the lazy or for the busy (typically restaurants) such deposits are a problem, for once disseminated through the wine they do have an adverse effect on quality. It is presumably for this reason that one of Burgundy's larger and most respected winemakers, Louis Latour, opens every bottle of older red wine, inserts a fine stainless steel tube and draws off the sediment before topping up, recorking and sending the wine off to England, the United States and Australia.

Max Schubert, the father of Penfolds Grange Hermitage and unquestionably one of Australia's greatest winemakers, took precisely the opposite view. He saw the sediment (or crust) of a red wine as an essential ingredient of quality. It is laid down in the vigorous youth of the wine, said Schubert, and is a storehouse of food and energy for its old age. He was adamant that the wine reabsorbs flavour from the crust as it ages, and is all the better for doing so. For this reason he experimented with chains, ball bearings and sand to score or scratch the inside of the bottles into which the early Grange Hermitages (1952 and 1953) went. The rough surface aided the throwing of the crust, but the labour-intensive treatment was necessarily discontinued once Grange came into commercial production.

White wines, too, can throw deposits. One of the most common, which can appear in relatively young wines as well as old, is tartrate crystals, which are white and like very coarse particles of sand or grit. These are harmless: they have neither a beneficial nor an adverse effect on quality, but once again uninformed opinion is against them. In reaction to this, German wine producers have imaginatively named the tartrate crystals 'wine diamonds' and made somewhat extravagant claims on back-labels about the quality they denote.

Old French white wines (white burgundies and very old Vouvrays are typical examples) can deposit an appreciable and easily visible fine, loose sediment. It is highly desirable to decant such wines just as if they were reds: while the effect is largely optical, a cloudy glass of white wine is not appealing. Modern techniques of cold stabilisation (which precipitates out the tartrates before bottling) and ultra-fine filtration largely eliminate white wine sediments, but the small or traditional winery may not use such procedures, so the problem has not disappeared altogether. (I discuss the service of old wines, both white and red, in Chapter 10.)

ageing and the changes in taste

Enough of the physical causes and indicia of the changes which occur in wines as they age: what happens to the taste of the wine? The answer to this question lies in one immutable law: from the moment a wine is placed into the bottle, there is a gradual, imperceptible (from one month to the next) but inevitable modification of the primary fruit flavour present in the wine at the start of its life. For a certain number of years — it may be one or two, it may be 20 or even 40 — the softening of and diminution in primary fruit flavour will be more than compensated for by the gain in secondary flavours. This fruit loss and complexity gain is the product of some extremely complex chemical changes. While a considerable amount is known about the organic chemistry involved, the interrelationship between that chemistry and what we actually taste is less clearly understood. Modern analysis techniques — gas chromatography mass spectrophotometry (GCMS analysis) coupled to a computer, infra-red spectrophotometry, nuclear magnetic resonance, and ultraviolet spectrophotometry — will undoubtedly provide the answers in time, but in any event are more suited to an oenology journal than a book of this kind.

the screw cap:
back from the grave?

Suffice it to say that the key element in this process is the polymerisation of anthocyanins, and here I must point out this process will take place even in a hermetically sealed container, such as a can or a sealed glass flask. The cork merely supplies additional oxygen over a period of time; even if nitrogen is bubbled (*sparged* is the technical term) through the wine about to be bottled, and even if the bottling line is nitrogen charged and the empty bottle filled with nitrogen before the wine is introduced, the process of ageing will go on regardless, thanks to the stored oxygen in the wine. So wine bottled with an ACI-Stelvin screw-on cap (a type of metal cap like those used on spirit bottles and often used on bottles of wine served on aircraft) will still age, but will do so more slowly than a wine with an average cork. (Over a period of five years in the 1970s I participated in an annual 'blind' or 'masked' evaluation of wines bottled with conventional corks and with Stelvins: there was no question that the Stelvin-capped wines were fresher, showed no cork taints, and were in fact better wines. Yalumba was sufficiently persuaded of this to bottle its first Pewsey Vale rhine rieslings with Stelvin closures; Reynella and Hungerford Hill also experimented with them. The public, however, wanted none of it and gave a resounding thumbs down. Twenty years later, and driven to the edge by the frustration of cork taint, the screw cap — along with other forms of closure — is once again being seriously trialled.)

from purple to red to brown

The oxygen present interacts with a number of substances: with the tannins and colouring matter (principally anthocyanins) and with the various acids naturally present in all wines. The tannins and anthocyanins are polymerised (a process which will also occur, albeit more slowly, in the absence of oxygen), leading to the colour change from purple in a young red wine through to brick red or tawny in an old red. The tannins are likewise polymerised (and thereby softened), and the by-products of this process then precipitate to form the crust or sediment which I have talked about earlier. For this reason a deeply coloured, tannic wine will usually live longer than a light-bodied one. It follows that over a very long period of time, the colour of red wine will steadily diminish in depth and intensity, ultimately reaching a pale onionskin colour in extremely old wines. All things are relative, however, and exceptional wines can retain strong colour for a century or more.

The other oxidation process is unseen, as it has no effect on the colour of the wine. This is the interaction of oxygen with acids to form aldehydes and esters. These provide the bouquet of a mature wine, which is quite different from the aroma of a young wine. Aroma derives from the primary fruit character of the grape, although the yeast used during fermentation may well mask or distort this aroma in very young white wines. If one opens a bottle of very old wine which has nevertheless been well corked, the changes in the bouquet will be both very marked and very rapid. Through long bottle-ageing, the wine will have been depleted of most of its oxygen, and will eagerly absorb it on opening. This will in turn liberate a volume of aldehydes, but these are typically short-lived and before long the chain breaks down, leading to a flat and oxidised old red. Timing the opening is thus all-important. (I discuss this at length in Chapter 10.)

white wine to yellow: still a mystery

Changes also occur in white wine, although the tannins present are infinitely lower and anthocyanins altogether absent, and the mechanisms of colour change are still not properly understood by research scientists. The oxidation process changes the colour from a light straw-green to a deep burnished gold (the very best wines will still retain tinges of green). The flavour progresses from crisply acid fresh fruit through a soft and voluptuous mid-age prime (the bouquets and flavours of toast, butter and honey are common) thence to the madeirisation of old wine and ultimately to a sherry-like quality. This was the flavour of a 1727 Rudesheimer Apostlewein (from Germany's Rheingau in the Rhine Valley) drunk in 1979, although a 1646 Hungarian Tokay tasted a few years later was quite extraordinary. The sweetness was only a memory, but the wine had remarkable freshness and strength.

the eternal question: when to drink this wine?

Obviously enough, the total transition from raw youth to extreme old age covers a span of years outside the everyday experience of the vast majority of wine-drinkers. The most commonly asked of all questions ('When should I drink this wine?' or 'When will this wine be at its best?') are set against a far shorter time-frame. And they are questions which cannot be answered unless a great deal of supporting information is supplied by the questioner for, at the risk of stating the obvious, what the questioner really means is 'When will I most enjoy this wine?', which is a largely subjective question.

Thus most French experts would give a far earlier range of dates than would the English, simply reflecting the fact that the French tend to drink their wines at a far younger age than do the British. If questioned, they would no doubt point to the fresh fruit and vibrant colour, aroma and taste of the young wine. These are the characters that afford the most pleasure. The English, and to an even greater degree Americans (and I suspect Australians), who revere the great wines of France, tend to cellar them for far longer. We would say the '70 and '71 Bordeaux are at their peak now; the '82s, '85s and the '86s some way off; the '90s unready; the '75s undrinkably tannic; the '78s just starting to show the first signs of drinkability; and the still precocious '89s needing to shed some puppy fat. This would all be nonsense to the average French drinker, who would have happily consumed all of those wines before now, and be contentedly moving his or her way through the '90s and '94s.

the first rule

So the first rule is to drink the wine when it most pleases you. One of the unforgivable sins — which I have committed all too often — is to open a bottle and say, 'Heavens, that is absolutely perfection: I must put the rest of the bottles away.' When you bring out the next bottle two, three or five years later, as like as not the magic will have gone or at least faded. Another rule is: a wine suitable for a hot summer's Saturday night when you are tired and thirsty will be very different from that required on a mid-winter's night before an open fire when your sole activity for the day has been the walk to and from the office parking station to deposit and pick up your car. Nor do the maxims stop there: your palate changes as you grow older and wine-wiser. What suited you last year is unlikely to give the same pleasure next year.

For all that, it is possible for experts to pick a mid-point, give an approximate span of years. The intelligent consumer will simply use the indicated drinking span as a yardstick, comparing his or her own reaction to the wine against the expert's recommendation. The result may be to add two or subtract three years from that recommendation; that is not to say either protagonist is right or wrong, merely that tastes and expectations differ.

Moss Wood Cabernet Sauvignon

Entirely estate-grown on a vineyard site which, even by the standards of Margaret River, is exceptional. It is rightly revered and eagerly sought.

assembling
the cellar

bloodlines and breeding

You may well feel that I have so far been long on generalisations and short on specifics. You have been persuaded it is worth starting a cellar, but do not know where or how to begin the process of selection.

The first thing to understand is that it is going to be a long, slow process unless you have suddenly struck it rich and have an unlimited budget. Even then, the instant cellar — impeccably selected by the greatest expert in the land and without regard to cost — will be less than perfect. We all have our likes and dislikes (logical and illogical), and never more so than with wine. Your expert can tell you what is a good wine, but he or she cannot tell you which particular wines you should prefer. So the cellar should grow with you, imperceptibly changing shape and direction as your wine knowledge grows, worn-out bits being discarded and other choices substituted.

advice and help:
there are many sources

If you live in one of the great cities of the world, the first step is to find a fine wine merchant and build a dialogue with him (in Australia at least, female merchants are all but unknown). By exchanging comments on particular bottles you have tried, the good merchant will quickly gain an understanding of your palate, be able to recommend certain wines and steer you clear of others. The other essential preliminary step is to subscribe to a specialist consumer wine magazine or access a good website. A short list and description of the major Australian, American and British magazines, together with subscription prices and details as at the end of 1997, appears in Appendix 5. A short list of the ever-expanding number of websites appears in Appendix 8. An increasing number of books performing the same function are also listed; Michael Broadbent's classic works *The Great Vintage Wine Book* (*I* and *II*) stand a little to one side as timeless reference works for the professional and for the seasoned amateur.

It will be apparent from my description of these magazines and books what each has to offer the reader, but a 'dialogue' of a different sort from that maintained with your wine merchant must be established. In other words, you cannot simply accept the recommendations and opinions you read as having any universal truth or validity. You must constantly test them against and relate them to what your own palate tells you. Particularly if you follow the writings of one expert, you will rapidly build up a sixth sense which tells you whether you are more likely than not to enjoy a particular wine.

This intelligent or 'live' use of written material becomes all important to the small-town or country dweller, whose access to a fine wine retailer is either infrequent or non-existent. The better retailers have informative price-lists-cum-bulletins, the most striking (and amusing) being that of Oddbins in the United Kingdom. Most Australian retailers have less elaborate bulletins, but these change far more frequently (usually on a monthly basis) with completely new editorial and tasting notes each issue.

first taste your wine

So these are the bases from which the process of choice may start. The first rule in taking the next step — the purchase — is to always taste the wine before buying it in quantity. Most Australian fine wine retailers have regular tasting programs, often co-hosted by the winemaker of one of the wineries being featured. The wine-lover living in Sydney or Melbourne would theoretically be able to attend free wine tastings every day of the week, with a weekly selection of upwards of 50 wines to choose from. Obviously enough, here you are able to taste the wine before you have spent a single dollar. Equally obviously, there will also be many hundreds — indeed thousands — of wines released each year where no such opportunity will present itself. In such circumstances, seek to buy a single bottle (while reserving a case or more, depending on one's budget) and drink it before confirming or cancelling your reservation.

Drinking the sample bottle may seem a straightforward matter, but the serious collector (for whom these rules remain equally valid) is apt to change it into an art form. The bottle will be opened in a tasting room (or at least in a room free of cooking or other extraneous smells) and approximately 50 millilitres poured into a tasting glass. The colour will be assessed and noted, a lengthy appraisal of the bouquet and aroma will follow, and then finally the wine will be tasted and, quite possibly, ejected into a spitting bucket. Speaking from first-hand experience, it becomes almost impossible to swallow a wine which is being tasted in this way, so used does one become to spitting in these circumstances. All of the characteristics of the wine will be entered onto a tasting sheet or into a computer, and kept as a permanent record.

Part of the wine may then be consumed with a meal. Further notes on the wine may be made at this juncture; it is quite extraordinary how much its character may appear to change. That change may be for the better, but it may be for the worse. Nonetheless, even at this stage, a final purchase judgement may not be made. Assume that half a bottle remains; it is then decanted into a clean half-bottle (to eliminate airspace) and the cork replaced. The process will then be repeated the following day, with variations on the procedure adopted on the first day. I know of a number of wine retailers who carry the process even further, deliberately leaving the wine in the original bottle (although replacing the cork) and tasting it over a period of three, four, or five days. This is the harshest test of all, and at some point will cease to be fair to the wine, which will inevitably start to deteriorate. But it does provide a storehouse of information which, if intelligently applied, can be of use in determining not only the present quality and style of the wine, but its likely future direction.

how much do you buy?

On the assumption that a decision is made to buy, the next question is, how much? If you are young, financial constraints will probably operate to limit the purchase to a dozen bottles (invariably called a case in the trade), and this is no bad thing for a learner. Unless the wine is fiendishly expensive, or unless it is unequivocally of a style which you are sure will not benefit from extended cellaring, a purchase of anything less than six bottles cannot be classed as a cellar purchase at all. If it is simply a purchase for current drinking, little more needs to be said. You will not have the opportunity either to repent at leisure or, more optimistically, to bask in the accumulating glory of the inspired purchase.

In Victorian times, the great cellars of England and Scotland assembled by nobility (which used to come up for sale from time to time through Christie's auctions in London) would quite frequently incorporate the purchase of 50 cases or more of a single wine, sometimes purchased in both bottles and magnums. The Royal Family, it seems, did things on an even grander scale: on Monday, 24 June 1901 (and on the four following days), at 'two o'clock precisely', Messrs Christie, Manson & Woods (by order of the Lord Steward) offered '5000 dozens of fine old bottled sherries, the property of Her Late Majesty Queen Victoria and His Majesty the King, being the overstock of wine purchased during the last century and prior to the year 1890, and now lying at the cellars at St. James' Palace, Buckingham Palace, Marlborough House, Windsor Castle and Sandringham'.

Times have changed, and for a private cellar one case is a reasonable purchase, two cases a substantial one and five cases an unusually large one. Assume the process of rigorous tasting and assessment of the sample bottle has been completed, and all the omens are good. The question still remains, how much to buy? Clearly, the answer will depend in large part on the life expectancy of the wine. I have much more to say on this issue in chapters 4 and 5 but, in general terms, bloodlines are as important in assessing the likely future performance of a wine as they are for a racehorse. Or, to use a well-known but nonetheless true cliché, the future may be read in the past. In many instances, you will be able to look back over 10 (or, in the case of French wines, 100 or more) prior vintages of the same wine and assess the potential of your new wine in the light of that prior performance.

In France, that prediction is enormously complicated by the impact of the particular vintage; in Australia and in the United States, vintage plays a significant role, but nowhere to the degree that it does in France.

Michael Hermitage past and present; one of Coonawarra's greatest names.

Milton Wordley/Wildlight

The bottling department at Lindemans, c. 1925, when their offices were situated in the Queen Victoria Building, Sydney.

Left: A wine auction in full swing at Christie's, London. *Courtesy Christie's*

Below: Catalogues from some of the major English and Australian wine auction houses.

The greatest sauternes of all — Chateau d'Yquem.
This bottle of Chateau d'Yquem 1784 was sold at
Christie's on 4 December 1986 for £39 600. Thomas
Jefferson's initials are engraved on the bottle.
Courtesy Christie's

Three bottles sold at Christie's 4 June 1987. From
left: a magnum of Chateau Lafite 1832 (£4400); a
jeroboam of Chateau d'Yquem 1937 (£7920); and
a magnum of Chateau Lafite 1848 (£4070).
Courtesy Christie's

chardonnay oak matured

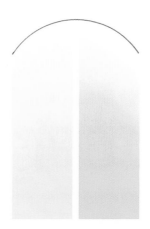

ONE TO TWO YEARS OLD

Light to medium-full yellow, hopefully with touches of green, grading in depth from the rim to the centre. Pink, brown, orange or grey tones — no matter how faint — are sure indications of problems, usually associated with oxidation but occasionally from poor oak. The yellow hues will range from lemon to buttercup from wine to wine. The darker the colour, the shorter the likely cellaring future, as the wine has probably been given extended skin contact prior to fermentation, a technique which gives added flavour and texture while young but which leads to coarseness in the medium term.

FIVE YEARS OLD

Medium to deep buttercup yellow. As with the one- to two-year-old wine, the lighter the colour, the more promising the wine, particularly if there is a little green tinge remaining. Whether medium or deep, there should be luminosity, as if a tiny light were buried somewhere inside it. Orange or brown aspects are unacceptable, and a sure indication of decay.

botrytised semillon & oak-matured (sauterne style)

TWO YEARS OLD

Although at the start of its life, each wine will show considerable variation because of different making techniques and philosophies. All such wines will be deeper in colour than a dry white of similar age, with a rich, glistening yellow hue lightening imperceptibly from centre to rim. An especially deep colour probably — though not inevitably — suggests the wine will reach full maturity very quickly.

FIVE YEARS OLD

As with the younger wine, the depth (and now the hue) will vary according to the maker. Ideally, the colour will be a golden yellow; sometimes distinct orange hues will have developed. If the wine glows with light, there need be no concern about orange tints, although the taste of the wine may suggest it is now fully mature. Strong 'legs', or slowly moving streaks of wine down the inside of the glass after it is swirled, are a feature of both young and mature wines of this type.

pinot noir

ONE TO TWO YEARS OLD

The colour will never be deep or dark; if it is, suspect the worst — the addition of 20% shiraz or cabernet sauvignon pressings, perfectly legal in Australia but totally inimical to the essential character of pinot noir. The hue should be purple/red, with the former rather than the latter dominant; graduation from the centre to the rim will be obvious. The wine should be brilliantly clear; if it is the slightest bit cloudy, or even more ominously, has a dull blackish tinge, all is not well. The blackish (or bluish) hue denotes excessively high pH, an old foe of pinot which leads to premature ageing.

FIVE YEARS OLD

Distinct onionskin tones will have developed, showing far more brown/brick hues than any other red wine of comparable age, and entirely off-putting to novices who have been taught that only reds and purples (preferably more of the latter than the former) are acceptable in red wine. The depth of colour, too, will be far less than usual — yet, as with all great wine, it will be clear and bright, with light penetrating through the depths of the glass as well as the rim. A pinot noir can turn quite brown, with all red hues excluded — and it is unlikely you will find such a wine giving you any particular pleasure.

shiraz & cabernet sauvignon

TWO YEARS OLD

I really doubt that anyone can differentiate these two wines on the basis of colour. A shiraz grown in one region may be lighter in depth and redder in hue than a cabernet sauvignon grown in another, but the difference will be as much due to regional as varietal influence. Taking a midpoint of these possibilities, the colour will be deep purple-red, almost impenetrable at the centre of the glass, and grading to crimson-purple at the edge. If the hue strays towards blue, or if there is a dull, blackish aspect to it, you have a high pH wine which will age quickly and without grace.

TEN YEARS OLD

Both the depth of colour and the hue will have changed. The depth will have lightened perceptibly, so that the graduation from centre to rim is less dramatic and the centre less profound. Purple will have given way to red (at the centre) and red to brick red (on the rim).

TWENTY YEARS OLD

This age will test most Australian wines, though the great vintages of Bordeaux will be just getting into their stride. Grange Hermitage, Coonawarra Cabernet Sauvignon and the top Hunters would be faring well. The progression from two to ten to twenty years will have continued, so that the colour will have lightened further. All traces of purple will have long since gone, and primary red hues will have been largely replaced by brick red, graduating to a warm tawny brown on the rim. There may be a substantial deposit, and unless great care is taken in moving the wine from cellar to table and then decanting it, minute flakes may appear suspended in the wine in the glass. This does not indicate a lack of quality in the wine, but rather in its service. The one requirement is that the colour has a healthy glow, that almost luminous sheen which is the hallmark of all great fully mature wine, be it white or red.

Chardonnay's progress: on the left, fermenting wine; in the middle, partially settled after five weeks; on the right, filter-bright finished wine.

There are no great old wines, only great old bottles. *Courtesy George Seper*

moving the goal posts: an extra challenge

Instead, the principal difficulties in assessing the potential of Australian and American wines stem from constantly changing approaches to both viticulture and winemaking. While the wine industry is 160 years old in Australia and older still in America, the fine wine industry in each country as we know it today can be said to date only from after the Second World War. Certainly, chardonnay and cabernet sauvignon (the white and red wines most in demand today) are essentially creations of the last 35 years in California, and the last 25 years in Australia. So, too, many of the winemaking and handling techniques widely used at the end of the 1980s were unheard of at the start of the 1960s and only sparingly used in the 1970s. This comment applies with particular force to American and Australian chardonnays: in both countries, chardonnays have by and large not repaid cellaring. (Chapter 4 provides more detail on the Australian scene.) I believe this is in part due to inherent deficiencies in the wine, but it also seems to stem from the year-by-year improvement in the young wines. In other words, the newly released chardonnay has a dual advantage: it has been made with greater skill (quite possibly from older vines) than in the past, and the fresh fruit character will often be more immediately appealing than the measured complexity of the older wine. So bloodlines have to be interpreted with as much skill and understanding as that of a bloodstock agent. If there is any doubt, I would suggest the purchase be limited to one case. It always seems that there will never be a better wine than the one you have before you; and the knowledge that unless you move quickly it will cease to be available is a further spur, but the reality is different.

service intervals: just like your car

After purchase, the wine should be allowed to rest for a minimum of two or three weeks, and longer if there has been a protracted period of transport — either from the other side of Australia, or from the other side of the world. The older the wine, the greater its need to settle down after transport. Old wines can take up to three months to recover fully from the effects of sudden movement. From then on, the wine should be periodically tasted against one's expectations. Obviously, a young, brawny and virile red which you expect to have a cellaring life of between five and 10 years can safely be left for three or four years, with perhaps only a passing examination to make sure there are no telltale signs of weeping through the cork and capsule. (I discuss periodic cellar maintenance checks and routines in far greater detail in Chapter 7.)

Once the wine approaches its expected peak (be that after a year or so in the case of a light-bodied white wine, or after five or more years for a full-bodied red), the time has arrived to start checking on progress by the only way I know (other than drinking someone else's stock): namely, opening and consuming the bottle.

Once again I have considerably more to say on the evolution of white and red wines in chapters 4 and 5, but I cannot emphasise enough that there is no magic moment at which a wine reaches its peak and at which it must be drunk. There is a process of improvement, leading eventually to a plateau (which, depending on the wine, can go on for many years or even decades) and finally the period of decline. Obviously, light-bodied red wines will develop, plateau and decline quickly, while full-bodied red wines will change with at times frustrating slowness. But even within this general pattern, there can be peaks and troughs on the way up, throughout the plateau, and on the way down.

growing up: adolescence, pimples and awkwardness

French folklore has it that wine in the bottle changes with the seasons, coming alive in spring. In bygone times, there was quite possibly a very sound biochemical reason for this: imperfectly filtered wines, which had been bottled before malolactic fermentation was complete, would start re-fermenting in the bottle as the warmer weather of spring arrived. The more romantic explanation was, of course, that the wine was responding to the regrowth of the vine from which it sprang. Less romantically, and rather more relevantly to modern-day wines, there is no question that at certain phases of a wine's development it can go through flat or awkward spots in precisely the same way as the adolescent suddenly bursts out in pimples or acquires embarrassing puppy fat.

In wine terms, this will occur in the intermediate phase, as it loses its primary fruit freshness and in its place gains the mellow complexity of maturity. The crossover point can be very difficult, with the wine showing neither fresh fruit on the one hand nor balanced mellowness on the other. Many a disappointed connoisseur has got rid of a wine at this stage, believing that he or she made a dreadful mistake in the first place, only to regret that decision with great bitterness five years down the track. The two wines that suffer most in transition are semillon and riesling, yet both emerge brilliantly.

wine retailers:
even bigger and better

As one's experience grows, so will the confidence to both buy and sell wine. The expert has three major sources when it comes to buying: retail, winery cellar door and auctions. During the 1990s there has been a fundamental change in the way wine is retailed in Australia, effectively copying earlier changes in the United Kingdom. Until the entry of the major supermarket chains into liquor merchandising, and in particular the establishment by Coles Myer of the Vintage Cellars chain of outlets, there was a simple choice. You could go to a small specialist retailer, receive advice, have access to a carefully selected range of wines, and expect to pay for that advice and expert selection. Alternatively, you could go to the early version of the supermarket, or the multiple outlets under single ownerships, and choose from a relatively limited range of heavily discounted wines, neither expecting nor receiving any guidance other than price.

Now the situation is infinitely better for the consumer. The independent specialist retailers still exist and deservedly do well; their range more exciting (and eclectic) than ever. But large chains such as Vintage Cellars and (on a smaller scale) The Grape in Brisbane now offer a superb range of wines at highly competitive prices and (usually) excellent advice.

A somewhat arbitrary list of merchants appears in Appendix 9. The tyranny of space means that many fine wine shops are not mentioned in this list: to these my apologies. Silence is not intended as an implied criticism.

cellar doors and mailing lists

The next major source is the winery cellar door and the winery mailing list. Depending on one's definition, there are between 780 and 830 wineries in Australia today. Ninety-eight per cent of the total Australian production comes from the 65 largest wineries; there are then over 700 wineries producing the remaining two per cent. This latter group includes over 500 wineries which either elect not to invoke the retail system at all or are willing but unable to have their wines sold by more than a handful of retailers, and even then usually with a very restricted geographic spread. The only way to purchase the wines of such producers is either to visit the cellar door, or to order off the mailing list.

The latter course has the problem that you are almost certainly buying without having first tasted and are more probably than not locked into an unbroken case buy. When freight costs are added on, it is not necessarily a bargain-basement buy either. Those wineries which do offer wine by both cellar-door/mailing list and through the retail system will usually seek to pitch their cellar-door price at 10 to 15 per cent below the nominal retail price. However, once one adds back the freight, and allows for the per case discount that is almost invariably available from the retailer, the two prices are one and the same.

The bigger the winery, the less attractive cellar-door purchase becomes: for the large companies, the house price (the price at which senior employees can purchase the wine from their company) often exceeds that offered by major discounters, and the cellar-door price is even higher again. This, too, can affect the smaller winery: some years ago an acquaintance returned from Western Australia, followed by a dozen cases or so of Margaret River wine. He had visited the Margaret River wineries, but had taken the precaution of pricing the wines at a major Western Australian retailer before he made the journey down from Perth to the Margaret River. Each wine was purchased at that retailer on his return to Perth at a price significantly below the cellar-door price tag. I have no doubt the same situation exists today. This, of course, can cause enormous resentment; sometimes it is the fault of the winemaker, but not always. Retailers have a nasty habit of suddenly slashing margins or dispensing with them altogether either to quit stock or to gain publicity. The winemaker has no control over such activities.

a special magic

For all that, there is a special magic in visiting the winery, talking to the winemaker and tasting and buying the wine on the spot where it was made. Indeed, the ambience can be altogether too much. There is an old saying in the English wine trade: buy on water and sell on cheese. In other words, in assessing the wine for purchase, do not allow any outside distractions; when selling, provide distracting tastes and surroundings. Similarly, a wine will never taste better than in the winery at which it was made; the winemaker's visible pride in his or her work is a potent medicine, making objective judgement all but impossible. This tendency, I might say, afflicts experts as much as it does amateurs, and the expert will always seek to have his opinion reinforced by a second tasting (preferably blind) conducted in the sterile confines of his work tasting room. For the amateur, the consequence of a mistake is nowhere near as dramatic: there is only a case or two to quit and, as I indicate later in this book, there are ways and means of achieving this.

auctions:
the greatest fun of all

The third method of buying wine is through auction. A substantial portion of my cellar was acquired this way, all the oldest French and German wines being purchased at Christie's in London — the majority during the golden days of the 1970s when auction prices were unbelievably low and the exchange rate incredibly favourable. (I say more about this in Chapter 9.)

A list of the leading English and Australian auctioneers appears in Appendix 3. All operate with roughly similar rules, most accepting absentee (mail, fax or phone) bids as well as bids from the floor.

The system works thus. Each lot has an estimate of price expressed as a range (typically a difference of 30 per cent between low and high) which is arrived at by reference to recent auction prices for the same or similar wine. The low end of the estimate is usually the reserve price below which the wine will not be sold, although room bidding may commence at a lower figure.

The highest mail or fax bid knocks out all other mail or fax bids, and will compete against bids from the auction room floor (and occasionally live phone bids, the last a cumbersome and difficult procedure). The bidding will be commenced by the auctioneer at either the first bidding step above the second-highest absentee bid or, if there are no absentee bids, at a price bid from the floor of the room.

While fair to the absentee bidders (whose bid is inevitably expressed as a *maximum*) the system can give rise to results which may at first sight appear strange, particularly when there are multiple lots of the same wine.

While some auctioneers spread absentee bids across the lots, others simply let the bids fall precisely as they arrive. Thus the first lot may bring a much higher price because it attracted a number of competing bids, whereas subsequent lots did not.

A second reason for the first lot sometimes bringing an abnormally high price is the convention observed by most auctioneers — that the successful bidder can elect to take all the remaining lots at the same price. Particularly for those present in the room, this can give rise to a form of Russian roulette for those who only want one lot, but want it quite badly. How far do you push the bidding on the first lot?

All auctioneers in fact recommend personal attendance at auctions, a perfectly sensible recommendation for rational or professional bidders. You can get the feel of the auction, take full advantage of unexpected bargains, and increase or decrease the tempo of your bidding according to your progressive success or failure (and your total budget). The problem comes for the amateurs or the enthusiasts who become infected with auction fever, and who become seemingly involuntarily engaged in a bidding duel which lifts prices beyond normal retail.

Theoretically, and in fact more often than not, auction room prices are equivalent to wholesale prices, even when the buyer's commission (ranging from 10 per cent in Australia to 15 per cent in England) payable to the auction house is added to the price. Auctions are also the main source of very old and rare wines: while retailers may be active purchasers, they tend to have specific customers in mind, and the wines will usually bypass the retailer's shelves.

Over the past 30 years some quite extraordinary sales have been held in London. The sale which started it all, and which in some ways remains the greatest, was held at Christie's on 31 May 1967. While now reverently known as the Rosebery Sale, it in fact offered wines from 'The Most Honourable The Marquess of Linlithgow, The Right Honourable The Earl of Rosebery and Kinghorn Kt, The Dowager Countess of Sandwich, The Right Honourable The Lord Bruntisfield', a colonel, a major and a mere wealthy widow.

Extreme rarities included an Old Hock circa 1780 (in a dumpy bottle), a 1740 Canary (in a rare bottle called, by glorious chance, a tappit hen), a 1757 Cape Wine from Holland, a 1750 Milk Punch, and an 1810 Malaga. The pre-sale tasting (free of charge) included 1858 and 1874 Chateau Lafite, 1874 Chateau Latour, 1865 Corton, 1857 and 1864 Sillery (the most famous champagne of the time), and 1886 Marcobrunner Auslese — the last of which I purchased a bottle of a decade or so later when it was resold through Christie's.

The core of the auction was the collection of Bordeaux wines from the golden age of claret, 1858 to 1878. There were 19 magnums and six bottles of 1858 Chateau Lafite. At the time of the sale Lord Rosebery said to Michael Broadbent: 'I do not entertain as much as I used to. I am too old for big dinner parties, and to open a triple-magnum for 16 or 18 people, of whom only one or two would *really* appreciate its rarity and beauty, would be a waste.'

There were other great auctions, too, notably the April 1970 sale of Sir George Meyrick's cellar at Hinton Admiral in Hampshire and the April 1971 Glamis Castle auction which disseminated treasure troves of phylloxera wines into the hands of connoisseurs and collectors around the world. It was Sir George Meyrick's cellar which provided the 1865 Chateau Kirwan, of which I have shared three bottles; two at Au Jardin des Gourmets Restaurant in London (in 1981), and the third at the 1995 Single Bottle Club Dinner in Australia (via resale at Christie's in 1994). It stands supreme as the greatest Bordeaux I have tasted, as rich and vital as a 20-year-old wine. I purchased the wine because I had read this account of the wine in Michael Broadbent's *The Great Vintage Book I* on the plane flight to London, and the words flashed before my eyes as I surveyed the wine list at Au Jardin only a few days later:

1865 Kirwan. A wonderful deep colour; lovely nose, sweet, fragrant, no signs of age or 'off' odours; slightly sweet, lovely flavour, perfect balance. An unusual find in the cellars of Sir George Meyrick. I do not make a practice of opening old wines in clients' cellars, but these bottles were unlabelled and unidentifiable. Happily the corks were clearly branded Kirwan 1865 and levels good. Sir George and I finished off the bottle for lunch. Another opened at the pre-sale tasting in October 1970 was identical.

In 1997 two modern-day collectors offered part of their cellars in auctions which recalled the Rosebery, Meyrick and Glamis Castle sales. The first was the Andrew Lloyd Webber Wine Collection auctioned by Sotheby's on 20 and 21 May 1997; and the second was an ostensibly anonymous vendor (widely believed to be the noted German collector Hardy Rodenstock) auctioned by Christie's on 18 and 19 September 1997. The Lloyd Webber sale realised £3.7 million, the Rodenstock sale £7 million.

The catalogues of each sale are works of art and collector's pieces in their own right, to be drooled over by disbelieving wine-lovers in another 30 years' time. It borders on the pointless to single out wines from either auction for special mention, but at the Rodenstock sale (for that is what I will call it) Chateau d'Yquems from 1847, 1858, 1864, 1865, 1869, 1870, 1872, 1884, 1888, 1890, 1891, 1893, 1895 and 1896 were all sold as introductions to a dazzling array of dozens of bottles of all the great vintages of the twentieth century.

Australian auctions are on a different scale, of course. While they regularly feature great French and other imported wines, their strength lies in Australian classics, and — most conspicuously — Grange Hermitage. Given the rarity of Grange of any vintage on retailer's shelves, the quantity and range of Grange to regularly come up for sales is quite surprising. Needless to say, other classics from Penfolds, Henschke (including Hill of Grace) and so forth regularly appear.

Langton's has always set the pace. It has introduced a silent bid auction, in which all bids are by mail or fax. The successful bid will be $1 per bottle higher than the second highest bid, and allows you to give complicated instructions not practicable at normal auctions — total spend limits, and reverse order bids (e.g. if bid for Lot 100 does not succeed, bid so much for Lot 50) and so forth.

Langton's has also pioneered a formal classification of Australia's finest wines into four categories: Outstanding (A), Outstanding, Excellent (A), and Excellent. Like the classification of the great wines of Bordeaux in 1855 into five growths (or crus), the rating is primarily based on auction prices.

It was first published in 1990, revised in 1996 and is due for further revision in 1999. Wines included in the classification must have a minimum of 10 vintages of production and a consistent record on the wine auction market. (With the permission of Langton's, it is reproduced in full in Appendix 10.)

However, all this causes me to utter a few cautionary words. There is no question that auctions can be a source of the greatest bargains and delights, but they also elevate the element of chance to the point where, truly, the auction should be extensively used only by experts. They are particularly valuable as sources of old and rare wines, but unless you are able to visit the auction rooms in advance and carefully inspect the bottles, the risk is obvious. Even inspection, and the usually scrupulously fair description of the condition of the wine (particularly as to ullage, something I have discussed in greater length in Chapter 2), provide a guide that may be as misleading as it is helpful. The consequences of poor cellaring are dramatic, but not always visible. What is more, the older and the rarer the wine, the less likely the buyer is to have any up-to-date, reliable information on its quality (in the sense of its present stage of development). Or, to put it succinctly, *caveat emptor*.

LEEUWIN ESTATE

1990

Margaret River

Chardonnay

PRODUCE OF WESTERN AUSTRALIA

Leeuwin Estate Chardonnay
In my judgement, this is the greatest of all the
Australian chardonnays and one of the few to
repay cellaring unequivocally for over a decade;
simply taste the '81, '82, '83, '85 or '87.

australian white wines for cellaring

O ne of the shibboleths of wine drinkers at large is that white wines do not repay cellaring. I can best answer that by pointing to the two oldest table wines I have drunk, a 1646 Tokay from Hungary and a 1727 riesling from Rudesheim in Germany. What is more, I remember reading of a German bockstein wine from around 1240 tasted during this century which was still sound.

If all this sounds like name-dropping of the worst kind, let me then argue that (French) white burgundies as a group age better than red burgundies. In other words, if I had a dozen different white burgundies and a dozen different red burgundies from a range of vintages since 1970, I think the white burgundies would comfortably outpoint the red burgundies; that more red than white wines would be tired and stale. Or to make another outrageous generalisation — that is the essence of generalisations, is it not? — no French sauterne worth the name should be drunk when it is less than 10 years old.

I believe that the vast majority of white wines benefit from some time in the cellar, but how much time, and with what result, are the real questions. Obviously enough, the answers will depend in large part on the grape variety involved; rather less obviously, but nonetheless importantly, they will depend on the winemaking techniques employed.

The last thing I would wish is to turn this into a technical treatise on winemaking, but it is necessary that I highlight the differences in the approach to making chardonnay of a typical (conservative) Burgundian and a typical (trendy high-tech) Australian.

The French winemaker will receive grapes grown on old, stunted vines planted at a density of 10 000 or more vines to the hectare and yielding around seven tonnes of grapes to the hectare. They will be crushed and pressed immediately, with a very substantial addition of sulphur dioxide. The juice may be allowed to settle in a large tank overnight, but whether or not this occurs, it will be quite milky (in other words, contain a very substantial percentage of suspended particles or solid matter left over from the skins and flesh) when it is transferred to barrel.

Fermentation will be allowed to start naturally, sometimes after a number of days has elapsed. It will then proceed at whatever temperature the cellar conditions permit; occasionally, heaters will be introduced to encourage the fermentation to start. Once under way, no cooling will be used, and even in small barrels the wine may well run past the 25 degree Celsius mark. At the end of fermentation the wine will be allowed to remain undisturbed except for periodic topping-up and a weekly or fortnightly agitation of the heavy lees deposited in the bottom of the barrel as the by-products of fermentation. Indeed, if it is a lesser wine and the proprietor is on friendly terms with a proprietor of one of the great estates, he may well seek to 'enrich' his wine by buying a little of the lees of a great wine and adding those lees to his barrels.

The wine will be allowed to remain in contact with the lees until the following spring, when it will be racked for the first time. One or two more rackings may follow before bottling, which usually (but not invariably) takes place late in the summer shortly before the next vintage. That decision will depend in part upon the amount of new oak used, and the wine may be allowed to rest past vintage and into the following winter before it is racked and (possibly but not necessarily) filtered prior to bottling. At all times the sulphur levels will have been maintained at a relatively high level.

The Australian winemaker will receive grapes from a relatively young vineyard planted at a density of around 1500 vines to the hectare and yielding 10 tonnes of grapes to the hectare. The grapes will be placed in a cool room overnight before crushing, and will then be placed in an airtight steel tank or press to remain in contact with the skins for between six and 24 hours. If sulphur dioxide is added, it will be in small quantities, and will very often be used in conjunction with ascorbic acid. The must will be chilled to maintain the temperature of 7 or 8 degrees Celsius at which the grapes emerged from the cool room. The must will then be pressed under gas cover in an air bag tank press, and the juice transferred to an insulated, jacketed tank where it will be allowed to cold-settle for 48 to 72 hours at around 5 degrees Celsius.

The brilliantly clear green juice will then be transferred to another stainless steel tank, in which an inert gas cover (nitrogen or carbon dioxide) is maintained. The juice will then be warmed up to around 15 degrees Celsius, and a carefully calculated dose of specially propagated yeast will be added. Once the yeast cell count has reached the desired levels — established by examining the juice under a powerful microscope — the temperature will be reduced to around 10 degrees Celsius and the wine allowed to ferment for anything between 15 and 25 days. The ideal will be to secure a drop in the sugar level of 0.5 baumé per day.

At some stage towards the end of the fermentation the wine may be transferred to oak barrels to finish its fermentation; part, indeed, may already have been transferred after only a limited period of time in steel, and fermented under strict temperature control in a cool room. More often than not, the wine will be racked and filtered shortly after fermentation, and the sulphur checked and carefully adjusted to ensure a free (uncombined) sulphur level of around 10 parts per million (once again, very low by French standards). The wine may then spend as few as three months in oak, and frequently will be blended and bottled within six months of the end of vintage.

If one then compares these wines one month after they are bottled, it will be difficult to believe they are made from the same grape. The French wine will be quite smelly (sulphurous), the colour will be a pale straw-green, there will be little or no obvious fruit in either the aroma or the palate, the texture will be hard, unyielding and chalky, and the finish no less aggressive.

The Australian wine will already be quite yellow, of a deeper and distinctively different shade from its French counterpart. It will already be quite aromatic, with pronounced oak aroma and flavour (even though it has spent less time in oak) and the palate will be soft, round and rich. 'Peaches-and-cream' is the expression I use to encapsulate the style. The wine calls out to be drunk immediately and, in all probability, the seduction thus accomplished will profit all concerned — the winemaker, the consumer and (if you wish) the wine itself.

The French winemaker started with far greater intensity of fruit flavour, but has subjected the juice to a variety of handling techniques which effectively subdue it, yet at the same time preserve its inner core of integrity. Sulphur is a powerful preservative, but it also retards development of vinous character until it is finally absorbed into the wine. Ten years or more after bottling, it will be possible to argue that the sulphur has contributed greatly to the complexity of the now fully mature wine. The Australian, on the other hand, was given far less fruit flavour to work with in the first place, but has done everything possible to polish and protect that flavour, enhancing it with new oak. But he has not prepared the wine for the harsh environment it confronts once it is removed from the protection of yeast lees, gas cover and temperature control. Certainly, it is placed in a bottle with a (hopefully) secure cork, but the ageing process which I have described in Chapter 2 has already begun its work. Most relevantly, the effects of the skin contact will rapidly manifest themselves: the already full colour darkens quickly, while the Mediterranean lusciousness of the peaches–and–cream teenager soon runs to ugly fat.

Each maker has approached his or her grapes with a carefully thought out and executed plan. The French winemaker is probably doing no more than following a tradition established by his or her ancestors many generations previously, and would be unaware that any other method of winemaking was possible. The Australian will have had to select from a bewildering array of options, and in all probability will jump like a cat on hot bricks from one combination of fermentation and handling techniques in one vintage to another in the next. But each in his own way has been correct. It is simply that the resultant style, and its need for cellaring, is radically different.

chardonnay

The history of Australian chardonnay in viticultural terms goes back to the early nineteenth century, to the days of James Busby and John Macarthur, two of Australia's earliest winegrowers. It is also quite certain that chardonnay wines were made in the nineteenth century, although surprisingly little record remains. Quite by chance, a few years before writing these words I was privileged to share in a bottle of Yeringberg

Pineau which, though it bore no vintage date, was almost certainly made sometime between 1900 and 1921, but it could conceivably have dated from the last years of the nineteenth century. It was served by Guill de Pury, whose grandfather had made the wine, and it was in remarkable condition, one of the greatest old white wines it has ever been my pleasure to drink. It had no doubt been helped by the fact that since it was purchased it had lain undisturbed in its original straw wrappers inside a wooden box in the chilly confines of a Tasmanian cellar.

The colour was golden yellow, while the bouquet was a wondrously rich amalgam of peach, honey, butter and nuts; there was no oxidation, and certainly no madeirisation. The promise of the bouquet continued with the taste of the wine; gorgeously soft peach, butter and honey flavours filled the mouth, before falling away ever so slightly with a very soft finish. The most remarkable feature of the wine was that it seemed to grow stronger and stronger in the glass; a small quantity saved throughout a three-hour period showed no sign of decay or collapse, and kept unfolding further sensations and flavours. The one thing that became more apparent was that 'pineau' indeed meant pinot chardonnay, the old-fashioned (albeit incorrect) name for chardonnay.

Murray Tyrrell: chardonnay renaissance

Isolated vineyard plots of chardonnay continued in production in the period between 1900 and 1970, but the variety was either unknown to, or ignored by, winemakers. The best-known plantings were in the Kurtz vineyard at Mudgee, and at Penfolds' HVD vineyard in the Hunter Valley. It was left to Murray Tyrrell to take the variety from obscurity and start a boom which shows no sign of slackening. In the late 1960s he procured cuttings from the HVD vineyard, and in 1971 (the worst Hunter Valley vintage in living memory, with continuous rain and appalling mould problems) produced the first Vat 47 Chardonnay. Throughout much of the 1970s, the Hunter Valley (with Murray Tyrrell to the fore) had chardonnay as its near exclusive preserve, but as South Australia slowly reacted and started to build up vineyard supplies in the latter part of the decade, the floodgates opened. It is a tribute to Murray Tyrrell that he continues to produce outstanding chardonnay under the Vat 47 label in the face of fierce competition from every corner of the land.

The amount of chardonnay being grown — and hence made — increased dramatically between 1979 and 1996, and is forecast to increase equally quickly until 1999, rising from 1000 tonnes in 1979 to 172 000 tonnes in 1999. As virtually every winemaker in Australia in virtually every possible combination of climate and soil has sought to mould this very complaisant variety into his or her image, chardonnays of strikingly diverse style have emerged. What is more, winemakers have gone through a steep learning curve as they have been able to look back over their shoulders to see how their earlier vintages have developed in bottle, and form a better view about the cellaring future of their wines.

The three faces of chardonnay

In the result, three distinct strands of chardonnay have developed. The first includes wines deliberately fashioned to bloom quickly and lusciously, inevitably fading or going to fat almost as quickly. These wines have a deep yellow colour by the time they are one or two years old, have extraordinary richness and often an almost viscous sweetness on the palate, and usually a generous dollop of oak. They have been made using a method called skin contact, which extracts flavour compounds and (it seems) colouring pigments from the skin of the grape. Utterly seductive after one year, such wines have carried the banner of Australian chardonnay around the world — but in my view they are usually unsuited to cellaring, as they quickly become oily, phenolic and heavy in the mouth.

In this strand, one also increasingly finds the new breed of cheap chardonnay, selling for the same price as riesling, semillon, or sauvignon blanc. Such wines typically come from high-yielding, Riverland vines grown in a very warm climate and which are totally reliant upon irrigation. These cheap chardonnays are made in a simple fashion, and such oak flavour as is present will most probably have come from the use of oak chips or inner staves rather than oak barrels. Such wines have their counterparts in all of the main varieties, red and white, and in no case should one expect that time in the bottle will turn a sow's ear into a silk purse. They start off life as simple wines with a modest amount of fresh fruit: all that will happen with time is simply that the freshness will fade without any compensating buildup of complexity.

The second style is very much the creation of the 1990s — unwooded chardonnay. When first introduced it became instantaneously fashionable and much in demand. After only a few years, however, the fascination waned as winemakers and consumers alike came to understand that unwooded chardonnay requires high quality grapes if it is to be consumed young, and that high quality chardonnay deserves (good) oak treatment. 'Ordinary' unwooded chardonnay makes an essentially bland wine, no bad thing in itself, but not calculated to set the pulse racing.

The third strand, accounting for only a small percentage of total chardonnay production, offers wines which either respond well to or positively demand cellaring. These are usually — though not necessarily — grown in cool climates, and even more probably come from relatively low-yielding vines. They are likely to be either whole-bunch pressed or have received nil or minimal skin contact, to have been barrel fermented, to have been matured in barrel on their lees, to have undergone partial or total malolactic fermentation, and will not have been rushed into bottle.

The more delicate, chablis-like of these wines start off life in the manner of a traditional young Hunter semillon: it takes either an article of faith or a knowledge of bloodlines and breeding to assume the wine will develop complexity, flavour and richness as it ages. Others start off at the opposite end of the spectrum, with concentration and viscosity in the mould of a Le Montrachet: once again, though, it takes experience (usually of prior vintages) to know such wines will not run to fat and to seed.

The following table is a little different to the others in this book. Obviously enough, there is no question about the cellaring potential of the wines in the right hand column. Those in the centre will, by and large, stand up to a year or two in the cellar, a few indeed offering improvement, others moving from varietal chardonnay to a regional or generic full-bodied white burgundy style. Which manifestation you prefer is essentially a matter of personal preference or prejudice, but you should taste such wines regularly to be sure you are happy with the way they are developing.

chardonnay

region	quality producers	wines with special cellaring qualities
new south wales		
Hunter Valley	Allandale, Brokenwood, Evans Family, McWilliam's, Pepper Tree, Petersons, Rothbury	Lakes Folly, Rosemount, Scarborough, Tyrrell's
Mudgee	Andrew Harris, Miramar, Montrose, Thistle Hill	
Orange	Bloodwood Estate, Canoblas Smith, Reynolds Yarraman, Rosemount	
victoria		
Geelong	Scotchmans Hill	Bannockburn
Gippsland	Narkoojee	Nicholson River
Macedon/Sunbury	Cleveland, Portree	Craiglee
Mornington Peninsula	Dromana Estate, Kings Creek, Main Ridge, Massoni, Moorooduc Estate, Paringa Estate, Port Phillip Estate, T'gallant, Willow Creek	Paringa Estate, Stoniers
North-East Victoria	Brown Bros	Giaconda
Pyrenees	Blue Pyrenees Estate	Dalwhinnie
Yarra Valley	Lillydale Vineyard, St Huberts, Seville Estate, Shantell, Yarra Edge, Yarra Ridge, Yarra Valley Hills, Yering Station	Coldstream Hills, de Bortoli, Tarrawarra, Yeringberg
south australia		
Adelaide Hills	Bridgewater Mill, Chain of Ponds, Grosset, Henschke, Hill Smith Estate	Mountadam, Penfolds, Petaluma, Geoff Weaver, Lenswood Vineyards
Barossa Valley	Grant Burge, Krondorf, Orlando, Peter Lehmann, Tollana, Wolf Blass, Yalumba	
Coonawarra	Brands, Rymill, Rouge Homme, Wynns	Katnook Estate
Padthaway	Thomas Hardy	Lindemans
Riverland	Renmano	
McLaren Vale	Andrew Garrett, Chapel Hill, Ingoldby, Maxwell, Norman's, Pirramimma, Seaview	Geoff Merrill, Wirra Wirra

chardonnay *continued*

region	quality producers	wines with special cellaring qualities
western australia		
Great Southern	Alkoomi, Gilbert, Goundrey, Karriview, Old Kent River, Pattersons, Wignalls	Howard Park, Plantagenet
Margaret River	Ashbrook Estate, Cape Mentelle, Devils Lair, Evans and Tate, Palmers, Vasse Felix, Voyager Estate	Cullen, Leeuwin Estate, Moss Wood, Pierro
Geographe		Capel Vale
canberra district		
Canberra District	Doonkuna Estate, Lark Hill	
tasmania		
Tasmania	Delamere, Freycinet, Heemskerk, Iron Pot Bay, St Matthias, Meadowbank, Moorilla Estate, Notley Gorge, Wellington	Pipers Brook

semillon

With semillon, the opposite is the case. Young, unadorned semillon is — quite frankly — not a particularly attractive wine. If your desire is for a totally neutral, bone-dry food carrier, then young semillon is a possibility. But modern-day palates are becoming increasingly seduced by forward chardonnays, sumptuously-oaked sauvignon blanc and botrytised riesling, all of which have an extremely pronounced aromatic profile. Place a simple semillon against any one of such wines and it will be lost. Place the same simple little semillon, unadorned by oak but given the benefit of 20 years in bottle, against its erstwhile victors and the result will be exactly the opposite: the other wines will be long since gone, fallen to fat and to seed, while the semillon will be there in all its glory, glowing golden and redolent of honey and well-browned toast.

Such, in any event, was the outcome for virtually any semillon made by Lindemans in the Hunter Valley in the 1960s; the Rothbury semillons made between 1972 and 1979 (other than the oaked styles, which are in a different category); Tyrrell's Vat 1 wines; and McWilliam's Lovedale (conspicuously) and Elizabeth, the last one of the great bargains of the Australian wine market.

A changing world

But it is a changing world. Rothbury had all but given up the effort of making a semillon even before being acquired by Mildara Blass, and there seems scant likelihood of any change in the future. Former makers such as Hungerford Hill and Tulloch have likewise sought other varieties (or other regions), while Lindemans sold or abandoned most of its great vineyards in the dark days of the 1970s and '80s.

On the credit side, Brokenwood has emerged as a significant producer; while most of its semillon is consumed young, winemaker Iain Riggs is consciously striving to produce a wine that will also age well. Lindemans, too, has signalled a desire to restore its former reputation, and has started a long-range programme designed to achieve this. Tyrrell's has added a significant dimension with a museum release program for bottle-aged Vat 1 semillons (at least five years old) and also with 'Futures semillon', likewise released when five years old. Just when it seemed aged Hunter semillon was doomed to extinction, it has attained a new — and richly deserved — lease of life.

Another manifestation of the changing world is the emergence of what might be termed the Margaret River style — semillon with a distinctly herbaceous aroma and taste. Quite why the Margaret River should produce such wines is not clear, because normally one would associate the character with a much cooler climate than the Margaret River in fact possesses.

Finally, there are the oaky wines which come both from classic areas such as the Hunter Valley and other regions such as the Barossa Valley which once ignored the potential of semillon. It is inherently unlikely that the mere introduction of oak (to bolster immature flavour) will change the long-term outlook for such wines — although the ageing capacity of semillon should never be underestimated.

Finally, there are the botrytised semillons, with de Bortoli standing supreme since it pioneered the style in 1982. These wines are usually released at four years of age, and will easily live for a decade: those of de Bortoli are of world class.

semillon

region	quality producers	wines with special cellaring qualities
new south wales		
Hunter Valley	Allandale, Marsh Estate, Petersons, Reynolds Yarraman, Rosemount, Tamburlaine	Brokenwood, Lindemans, McWilliam's, Rothbury, Tyrrell's
Young	Hungerford Hill, McWilliam's	
Murrumbidgee Irrigation Area	Wilton Estate	de Bortoli
victoria		
Yarra Valley	de Bortoli, Yarra Yering	
Gippsland	Narkoojee	Nicholson River
south australia		
Adelaide Hills	Chain of Ponds	
Barossa Valley	Basedow, Grant Burge, Penfolds, Peter Lehmann, Tollana	
Clare Valley	Tim Adams, Mitchell, Quelltaler	
western australia		
Margaret River	Cape Clairault, Cape Mentelle, Chateau Xanadu, Voyager Estate, Willespie	Ashbrook Estate, Evans & Tate, Moss Wood

riesling

Riesling may be less popular than it once was, but it is still the second most important white wine in Australia, with more bottles sold each year than of all the other white varieties (other than chardonnay) grouped together. Most of it is made as dry, or near-dry, table wine. In this guise the commonly accepted view is that it does not repay cellaring. Yet one only has to look at the great old Leo Buring White Label Reserve Bin rieslings to know that this generalisation is as misleading as most. In April 1997 I was privileged to participate in a tasting of 30 Leo Buring rieslings dating back to 1963 presided over by John Vickery, who made them all.

The 1966, 1967, 1970, 1971 and 1972 vintages were absolutely superb, glowing with an intense yet lively buttercup-gold colour as they were poured, rich in lime/toast aroma, and with extraordinary vinosity (viscosity, almost) on the palate.

Even more remarkable are the very old rieslings which somehow or other have survived the passage of time in the Yalumba private cellars, and which are brought out from time to time for the museum tasting Yalumba holds in conjunction with the biennial Barossa Vintage Festival. Over the past decade I have tasted wines from 1934, 1939, 1940, 1942 and 1944 — the 1934 G29 Riesling Bin C046 being not only the oldest but one of the greatest. Writing in *The Australian Wine Compendium* (Angus & Robertson Publishers, 1985) of a tasting that included that wine, I had this to say:

1934 G29 Riesling Bin C046 is one of the oldest rhine rieslings still left in the Barossa Valley. Oldest it may be, but it was also one of the outstanding wines in the grandmother group. The bouquet was clean, with a touch of camphor (but no oxidation or volatility) and still retained fruit fragrance and aroma; the palate is drying but firm, with identifiable riesling fruit flavour. It was a truly glorious bottle.

Yet another tasting, held some years earlier in October 1978, showed that humble commercial riesling could also defy accepted wisdom. Orlando staged a silver anniversary tasting of Orlando Barossa Rhine Riesling covering every vintage between 1953 and 1978. The outstanding wines in the line-up were 1953, 1954, 1958, 1960, 1961, 1962, 1966, 1968, 1973 and 1977. The outstanding single wine was 1954 Bin B, a blend of Barossa Valley and Eden Valley fruit. Gloriously fresh, and with that typical Eden Valley lime-juice character, it seemed more like a five-year-old than a 25-year-old wine.

Nonetheless, I would be the first to agree that most riesling will give maximum enjoyment in the 12 months following its release (typically that release will take place towards the end of the year in which the wine was made, giving an approximate two-year span); and, secondly, that aged dry riesling is something of an acquired taste. For those who wish to develop that taste, or simply see what happens, the table will point you in the right direction.

Since 1980, botrytised rieslings with very substantial residual sugar (ranging from auslese to trockenbeerenauslese sweetness and weight on the German scale) have become increasingly common. These most certainly require a year or so in bottle to start to show their best, and some should have a long life in front of them. The absence of a track record makes it difficult to be dogmatic, although one of the forerunners, Brown Brothers' 1970 Milawa Spatlese (now called Noble Riesling), drank well until the end of the 1980s. One or two of the new generation wines (far more heavily botrytised and hence sweeter) have tended to develop at an alarming pace, and likewise to become a little broad and flabby, so generalisations are difficult.

riesling

region	quality producers	wines with special cellaring qualities
victoria		
Central Goulburn Valley		Mitchelton
Central Victorian High Country	Delatite	
Great Western	Seppelt	
North-East Victoria	Brown Bros	
Yarra Valley	de Bortoli	
south australia		
Adelaide Hills	Glenara, Heggies, Henschke, Orlando	Ashton Hills, Geoff Weaver, Pewsey Vale
Barossa Valley	Grant Burge, Rockford, Wolf Blass	Leo Buring, Orlando, Peter Lehmann, Richmond Grove, Tollana
Clare Valley	Brian Barry, Eldredge, Jim Barry, Leasingham, Paulett, Pikes Skillogalee, Sevenhill, The Wilson Vineyard, Waninga	Grosset, Mitchell, Petaluma, Knappstein Wines,
Coonawarra	Hollick, Lindemans	Katnook Estate, Wynns
McLaren Vale	Wirra Wirra	
Padthaway	Lindemans, Seppelt	

riesling *continued*

region	quality producers	wines with special cellaring qualities
western australia		
Geographe		Capel Vale
Great Southern	Castle Rock Estate, Chatsfield, Forest Hill, Frankland Estate, Galafrey, Gilbert, Jingalla, Goundrey Plantagenet	Alkoomi, Howard Park, Karrivale, Tingle-Wood
Margaret River	Leeuwin Estate	
tasmania		
Northern Tasmania		Pipers Brook
Southern Tasmania	Wellington, Winstead	Moorilla Estate

sauvignon blanc

Sauvignon blanc has its detractors in Australia, as it does in most parts of the world — those people inclined to describe it as 'cat's pee under a gooseberry bush'. The Australian tristesse with the variety has been accentuated by the unquestioned excellence of New Zealand's sauvignon blanc, to the point where at one stage many observers — myself included — wondered why we in Australia should bother with the wine at all.

However, the situation has changed significantly during the 1990s. In 1990, 8555 tonnes were crushed in Australia; in 1999 it is expected over 19 500 tonnes will be harvested, which will not satisfy the demand (for over 20 000 tonnes). To put this into further perspective, the Australian crush of chardonnay did not exceed 20 000 tonnes until 1988. So it is quite clear there is significant marketplace acceptance of sauvignon blanc.

This has gone hand-in-glove with a significant refinement of and improvement in the style of the wine. The best sauvignon blancs are now grown in cool to moderate climates (notably the Yarra Valley, Padthaway, Coonawarra, McLaren Vale, Adelaide Hills, Margaret River and Great Southern) and are either fermented in stainless steel or accorded brief or partial barrel fermentation. The blending in of semillon is not uncommon, particularly in the Margaret River, and it is this region which is most likely to produce sauvignon blanc capable of ageing satisfactorily.

However, the cardinal rule for most sauvignon blancs is to drink them while young and fresh. If you are determined to cellar some, try Cape Mentelle, Katnook Estate or Shaw and Smith.

other white wines

The other white varieties are chiefly what are termed aromatics, and have little place in a planned cellar. Yet it is perfectly true that in my cellar I have such wines as more or less accidental survivors from bygone days — wines such as 1959 Seppelt Great Western Riesling Tokay, 1956 Great Western Chasselas Chablis Bin M14, Penfolds 1966 Rooty Hill Traminer, and 1981 St Leonards Late Harvest Chenin Blanc. So do not be intimidated: the odd bottle left over here or there may be more than a mere curiosity in 10 or 20 years' time.

SPECIMEN

Penfolds

Grange Hermitage

BIN 95

VINTAGE 1986   BOTTLED 1988

Grange Hermitage is generally recognised as Australia's finest red wine and has received international acclaim. This great wine developed by Max Schubert, commencing with the 1952 vintage, is made from premium Hermitage grapes grown at selected vineyards in South Australia and matured in small oak casks prior to bottling.

During an extensive tour of the Bordeaux region of France in 1950, Max Schubert studied numerous wine-making practices that have now become an integral part of Penfolds wine-making technique. He also observed the practice of maturing wine in new oak casks, a method previously untried in Australia. The development of Grange Hermitage represented the beginning of a new era in Australia's red wine making tradition.

This knowledge combined with Max Schubert's foresight, skill and dedication has resulted in Grange Hermitage, the definitive Australian dry red table wine, acknowledged to be amongst the world's classic wine styles.

It is recommended that Grange Hermitage should always be decanted before serving.

Bottled by PENFOLDS WINES PTY. LTD.

PENFOLDS WINES PTY. LTD., 534 PRINCES HIGHWAY, TEMPE, N.S.W. 2044. PRESERVATIVE (220) ADDED.

750ML WINE MADE IN AUSTRALIA 13.7% ALC/VOL

Penfolds Grange

Without question, this is the most collectible of all Australian wines, and sought throughout the world. It will continue to be the bellwether for Australia's fine wine prices.

australian red wines for cellaring

hile I have mounted what I hope is a convincing case for cellaring more than a token quantity of white wine, there is no question that the heart of a great cellar is red. Red wine is the most complex of all, and responds most to the ageing process which I have discussed elsewhere. The colour changes are dramatic: from the vivid purple of extreme youth, to the red-purple of a young but now complete wine, on to the dark red of a wine in its full prime, thence to the brick hues of an old wine, and finally to the fragile clarity of the centurion's tawny hues.

The changes in the aroma follow a similar path. In a young wine, oak, fruit and tannin are all there in abundance, with the varietal characteristics obvious to even the most casual observer. As the wine mellows, harmony comes first, followed by a build-up of complexity. Varietal dominance pure and simple may become blurred by regional character, while the style of the vineyard may become progressively more pronounced.

As the wine reaches its peak, so does complexity and, with it, an at times amazing array of bottle-developed scents: cedar chests, cigar boxes, a whiff of field mushrooms, hints of dark chocolate, the forest floor, echoes of the dark red berries of the wine's youth, camphor — the list goes on and on. With old age, the once razor-sharp definition of the bouquet disappears altogether, and only a few of the complex scents of the fully mature wine will remain. Even the expert can be uncertain of the variety or the district (or indeed country) of origin.

A great old wine will nonetheless have a bouquet which is at once ethereal yet intense, an almost sublime elegance which defies both logic and description. When I first smelt the bouquet of a bottle of 1938 Romanée-Conti 15 years ago (the greatest of all red burgundies and from my birth year) the tears were pouring down my cheeks before I knew what had happened. It was a totally involuntary reaction: primarily happiness, yet a curious edge of sadness at such perfection. (I should add the wine was at the peak of its power; no fading beauty there.)

tannins: balance is all-important

Since one learns most about a red wine from its bouquet, it comes as no surprise that the development of the palate should go along similar lines. The major difference lies in the impact of the tannins (be they oak- or fruit-derived) and to a lesser degree in the acid balance of the wine. It may well be that tannins do not have any odour in isolation, but I swear it is possible to anticipate their presence by reference to the bouquet. However that may be, they have a profound influence on the flavour and structure of all red wines. True it is that this impact will be least in the case of pinot noir and greatest in the case of cabernet sauvignon (with shiraz not far behind cabernet), but tannin almost invariably makes its presence felt in a young red.

If it does not make its presence felt, it means the wine has deliberately been made to be drunk immediately in the manner of a light-bodied white wine, and that it will have no cellaring future whatsoever. (Even beaujolais has tannin, albeit very soft and simply providing the lightest of structure for the wine.) On the other hand, massive, mouth-gripping tannin in a young red wine is no indication of future greatness. Any wine, white or red, young or old, must be balanced: in the case of a young red, the component parts may be disjointed and lack harmony, but one must feel confident that as the tannin softens, so will the fruit come up.

Both Californian and Australian (though relatively few French) red wines can be massively over-extracted. The warm climate prevailing in many of the Californian and Australian wine-growing regions produces berries which are thick-skinned and high in both anthocyanins and tannins. The cooler the climate, the lesser the development of tannins, and the less the risk of over-extraction.

Tannin will and does soften as the wine ages, but it must not be present in such levels as to outlast the fruit flavour, which also declines with age. The wines of Bordeaux of 1937, 1957 and 1975 were all too tannic.

flavour change: the swing of the pendulum

The ageing of the fruit flavour is interesting. Flavour appears to build up during the maturation phase, but also to become more round and fleshy. It then slowly sheds that fat, becoming finer and lighter, a stage not infrequently accompanied by the formation of the crust deposit in the bottle. Contrary to what one's palate appears to discern, acid levels do not change as a red wine ages: we talk about the acid softening, and so it appears, but in truth it is other chemical and organoleptic changes which have occurred and which interact to make it appear that there has been a change in the acid level.

There is no finite limit to the time these changes can take. However, the phase of extreme youth is often over in two years, and seldom extends beyond five years. The maturation phase, as the wine builds to its optimum, is rather more variable, ranging from two or three years to over 25. The plateau phase will be shorter if the wine reached it via the fast track, longer if the wine took its time to reach the plateau in the first place. Again, a very wide span (three to 30 or more years) occurs in the length of the plateau itself.

As wine slowly declines, bottle variation makes generalisations useless: as I have said elsewhere, there are no great old wines, only great old bottles. It is no accident that the vast majority of the pre-phylloxera wines which come onto the auction market in England are Bordeaux reds fashioned primarily from malbec and cabernet sauvignon. These wines, all at least 100 years old, have frequently stood the test of time with surprising and at times quite unbelievable grace.

the greatest bottle?

I am often asked, 'What is the greatest bottle of wine you have drunk?', to which I invariably provide a convoluted reply, simply because there is no easy answer. But one of the very greatest red wines I have drunk was 1865 Chateau Kirwan; I drank two bottles (on separate nights) at Joseph Berkman's London restaurant, Au Jardin des Gourmets, in the late 1970s.

The second of the two bottles did show some signs of age, notably a slightly earthy/mushroomy edge to the aroma and flavour. The first bottle, however, was sheer perfection: the colour (similar in both bottles) was still dark red, and the richness of the fruit flavour was more appropriate to a 20-year-old wine than a 110-year-old bottle. Indeed that first and perfect bottle was shared with a legal friend who flatly refused to believe it could be genuine; the second bottle was shared with Anders Ousbach, who went into transports of delight. If only I could have swapped the order of service of those two bottles: my legal friend would have gone away content, while Anders Ousbach would still be sitting in a trance at the restaurant refusing to move.

cabernet sauvignon

For all this, we know less about the cellaring capacity of Australian cabernet sauvignon than we do about shiraz. The fact is that cabernet sauvignon is essentially an invention of the 1960s and 1970s: in 1958 only 230 tonnes of cabernet were crushed in Australia, compared to 15 824 tonnes of shiraz and 32 228 tonnes of grenache. As the red wine boom of the 1960s surged, so did plantings, but the vines were young and — in the face of insatiable demand — the 80 per cent rule (that a wine could be called cabernet sauvignon if it contained 80 per cent cabernet sauvignon in its make-up, a requirement since increased to 85 per cent, incidentally) was stretched to quite unacceptable limits. So, in the outcome, not until the early 1970s did true cabernets become available in anything more than token quantities.

There are, of course, cabernets from earlier times: Thomas Hardy's wonderful reserve bin series wrought by Roger Warren and incorporating cabernet from the Southern Vales, Coonawarra and Tahbilk; the early Wynns Coonawarra Estate Cabernet Sauvignon from the mid-1950s (although there has always been a question mark as to how much cabernet these wines in fact contained); the old Tahbilk cabernets; and even older and rarer bottles such as the 1930 Hunter River Cabernet (made by Wyndham Estate and bottled by Matthew Lang & Co.), which was ultimately responsible for Max Lake reintroducing cabernet sauvignon to the Hunter Valley. Just to confuse the picture further, that wine was in fact a 50/50 blend of cabernet sauvignon and petit verdot.

Reynella, Penfolds and Seppelt also offered the occasional cabernet sauvignon. These wines have all aged beautifully, but they were made in tiny quantities by the master craftsmen of their time. Only the Reynella cabernet sauvignons were available on the market generally at the time of their release.

What, then, of the wines of the 1970s? I well remember an article written by wine merchant David Farmer which appeared in the newsletter produced by Farmer Brothers (formerly one of Australia's leading retailers) in which Farmer strongly argued that the majority of Australian reds had failed to develop in bottle as well as had been expected. I still incline to agree with that view, and think that some of the same factors as apply to chardonnay (page 39) have been at work. Equally, however, with well over 75 000 tonnes of cabernet now being crushed around Australia each year, there are many wines being made which are far more likely to repay cellaring than not, and these are listed below. Any such list is bound to give rise to injustices, whether by inclusion or omission, but at least it represents a starting point for the selection of an Australian cellar of cabernet sauvignon.

cabernet sauvignon

region	quality producers	wines with special cellaring qualities
new south wales		
Hunter Valley	Petersons, Reynolds Yarraman, Rosemount Estate	Brokenwood, Lake's Folly
Mudgee	Andrew Harris, Botobolar, Miramar, Thistle Hill	Huntington Estate
Young	Allandale, Hungerford Hill, McWilliam's Barwang	
victoria		
Bendigo	Passing Clouds	Balgownie
Goulburn Central and North	Osicka, Mitchelton, Mt Helen	Chateau Tahbilk
Geelong	Bannockburn	

cabernet sauvignon *continued*

region	quality producers	wines with special cellaring qualities
Great Western	Best's	Mount Langi Ghiran, Seppelt
Macedon/Sunbury	Hanging Rock, Knight Granite Hills	Virgin Hills
Mornington Peninsula	Dromana Estate, Karina, Moorooduc Estate, Stoniers	
North-East Victoria	Baileys, Boyntons of Bright	Brown Bros
Pyrenees	Mount Avoca, Summerfield, Warrenmang	Dalwhinnie, Redbank, Taltarni
South-West Victoria		Seppelt Drumborg
Yarra Valley	Coldstream Hills, de Bortoli, Oakridge Estate, St Huberts, Seville Estate, Yarra Burn, Yarra Edge, Yarra Ridge	Arthurs Creek Estate, Mount Mary, Yarra Yering, Yeringberg

south australia

Adelaide Hills	Mountadam	Henschke
Barossa Valley	Elderton, Grant Burge, Krondorf, Orlando, Peter Lehmann, Rockford, Tollana, Yalumba	Penfolds, Seppelt, Wolf Blass Wines
Clare Valley	Eldredge, Jim Barry's Wines, Jud's Hill, Knappstein, Leasingham, Pikes, Quelltaler, Sevenhill, Taylors, The Wilson Vineyard	Grosset, Mitchell, Wendouree
Coonawarra	Balnaves, Hollick, Leconfield, Majella, Mildara, Rosemount Estate, Rouge Homme, Rymill	Bowen Estate, Brands Laira, Katnook Estate, Lindeman, Parker, Penley Estate, Petaluma, Wynns, Zema Estate
McLaren Vale	Coriole, d'Arenberg, Normans, Reynell, Richard Hamilton, Seaview, Wirra Wirra, Woodstock	Chapel Hill, Geoff Merrill, Thomas Hardy

cabernet sauvignon *continued*

region	quality producers	wines with special cellaring qualities
western australia		
Great Southern	Plantagenet	Alkoomi, Goundrey, Howard Park
Margaret River	Cape Clairault, Chateau Xanadu, Redbrook, Redgate, Voyager Estate, Willespie	Cape Mentelle, Cullen, Devils Lair, Leeuwin Estate, Moss Wood, Vasse Felix
Geographe	Capel Vale	
Swan Valley	Houghton, Lamont Wines, Olive Farm, Westfield	
tasmania		
Northern Tasmania	Marions Vineyard, Rotherhythe	

shiraz

Shiraz, or hermitage as it often used to be called, was for much of this century the premium red wine grape. Lesser-quality red wine was made from grenache or mourvedre, the plantings of which far exceeded those of shiraz.

As the tonnage of cabernet sauvignon doubled between 1983 and 1993, and as that of shiraz actually declined over the same period, it seemed inevitable that shiraz was doomed to become the poor cousin of cabernet sauvignon. Yet those statistics have been proved to be damned lies, for hidden behind them were fundamental changes which date back to 1984.

In that year a large group of English Masters of Wine came to Australia on a lengthy study tour. They returned to the United Kingdom overflowing with enthusiasm for Australian wine in general, and shiraz in particular. At that time Australian wine exports to the United Kingdom amounted to a paltry 600 000 litres per annum. By the end of September 1997 they were 75 000 000 litres, and the value per litre had trebled — a 4000 per cent increase in annual value.

But none of this happened overnight. While the enthusiasm of the MWs for shiraz was unbounded, the initial growth of Australian wine exports was based firmly on chardonnay and cabernet sauvignon in both the United Kingdom and United States markets. It was not until the 1990s that the consuming public began to take heed of the paeans of praise heaped on Australian shiraz by wine writers, educators, consultants and retailers around the world, and which reached a crescendo when the *Wine Spectator*, the world's most influential wine magazine (see Appendix 3), rated 1990 Penfolds Grange Hermitage first among its Top 100 wines from around the world in its December 1996 annual review.

No small measure of this resurgent popularity stems from the fact that, outside of France, there has been no significant competitor or alternative source of shiraz — unlike chardonnay or cabernet sauvignon. In the international wine market distinctiveness is a valuable commodity, and Australian shiraz (in its traditional guise, at least) can fairly be described as unique.

The net result of all this is that shiraz has thrown off the challenge of cabernet sauvignon, and has been planted at a greater rate than cabernet during the 1990s. Thus the projected crush of shiraz for 1999 is 141 000 tonnes compared to 101 000 for cabernet sauvignon.

And if anyone should doubt the ability of shiraz to age magnificently, I can only refer them to the vertical tastings in *Classic Wines of Australia, 2nd edition* (see Appendix 6). Here you will find detailed tasting notes for Best's Great Western Hermitage 1962–1994, Craiglee Hermitage 1979–1996, Eileen Hardy Shiraz 1970–1995, Brokenwood Graveyard Hermitage 1983–1994, Tahbilk 1860 Vines 1979–1992, Coriole Shiraz 1970–1994, Henschke Hill of Grace 1959–1993, Lindemans Hunter River Shiraz 1959–1992, McWilliam's Mount Pleasant O'Shea 1937–1954 (two series of tastings), McWilliam's Mount Pleasant OP and OH 1967–1994, Penfolds Grange 1951–1992 (two series of tastings), Penfolds Kalimna Bin 28 1971–1994, Penfolds Magill Estate 1983–1993, Penfolds St. Henri 1966–1993, Seppelt Great Western Colin Preece Dry Reds 1925–1962 (principally or partially shiraz), Seppelt Show Sparkling Burgundies 1944–1991, Seppelt Great Western Shiraz 1954–1993, St. Hallett Old Block Shiraz 1980–1994, Woodley Coonawarra Treasure Chest Claret 1930–1956 (two series), Wynns Coonawarra Estate Hermitage 1953–1995 and Wynns Ovens Valley Shiraz 1955–1992.

Many other wines from other varieties are also included in *Classic Wines*, but the foregoing is a roll call of honour for Australian shiraz — and for its longevity, and equally for its diversity of style.

shiraz

region	quality producers	wines with special cellaring qualities
new south wales		
Hunter Valley	Draytons, Marsh Estate, Petersons, Rosemount, Rothbury, Sutherland, Tamburlaine, Tulloch	Brokenwood, Lindemans, McWilliam's, Tyrrell's
Mudgee	Andrew Harris, Botobolar, Steins	Huntington Estate, Miramar
Young	McWilliam's Barwang	
victoria		
Bendigo	Balgownie, Passing Clouds	Jasper Hill, Mount Ida
Central Goulburn	Longleat, Mitchelton, Paul Osicka	Chateau Tahbilk
Geelong	Bannockburn, Idyll	
Great Western		Best's, Mount Langi Ghiran, Seppelt
Macedon/Sunbury	Cobaw Ridge, Hanging Rock, Knight Granite Hills	Craiglee
Mornington Peninsula	Paringa Estate	Merricks Estate
North-East Victoria	Boyntons of Bright, Brown Bros, St Leonards	Baileys
Pyrenees	Redbank, Summerfield, Warrenmang	Dalwhinnie, Taltarni
Yarra Valley	de Bortoli, Seville Estate	Yarra Yering
south australia		
Adelaide Hills		Henschke
Barossa Valley	Burge Family, Charles Melton, Elderton, Grant Burge, Peter Lehmann, Saltram, Turkey Flat, Wolf Blass	Penfolds, Rockford, St Hallett, Yalumba
Clare Valley	Leasingham, Mitchell, Paulett, Pikes, Sevenhill, Skillogalee, Tim Adams	Jim Barry Armagh, Wendouree
Coonawarra	Brands Laira, Penfolds, Rouge Homme, Rymill, Zema Estate	Bowen Estate, Lindemans, Wynns

shiraz *continued*

region	quality producers	wines with special cellaring qualities
McLaren Vale	Chapel Hill, Fox Creek, Haselgrove, Kay Bros, Maxwell, Normans, Richard Hamilton, Tatachilla, Wirilda Creek, Wirra Wirra, Woodstock	Chapel Hill, Clarendon Hills, Coriole, d'Arenberg, Hardys, Maglieri, Rosemount Estate

western australia

region	quality producers	wines with special cellaring qualities
Great Southern	Chatsfield, Goundrey, Gilbert Jingalla	Alkoomi, Chatsfield, Pattersons, Plantagenet
Margaret River	Evans and Tate	Cape Mentelle, Vasse Felix
South-West Coastal Plain		Peel Estate
Swan Valley	Evans and Tate	

canberra district

region	quality producers	wines with special cellaring qualities
Canberra District	Clonakilla	

queensland

region	quality producers	wines with special cellaring qualities
Granite Belt	Bald Mountain, Ballandean Estate, Kominos, Stone Ridge	

pinot noir

In the first edition of this book it seemed that I dismissed pinot noir as a cellaring proposition. The reason is (and was) I am concerned that pinot noir should not be cast in a false light: it is not a wine which by nature needs the time that a top cabernet or shiraz requires to show its best. Pinot noir should have an intense, fragrant, fruity bouquet, and a supple, fruity palate with a long finish and aftertaste, but relatively little tannin. While there are always exceptions which prove the rule, it is most likely that in Australia (and, for that matter, in the majority of Burgundian vintages) those qualities will be most apparent in the first five to seven years of the wine's life.

What is more, a good pinot noir does not need time to soften before it can be enjoyed: great pinot can be drunk while it is young in a way great cabernet cannot (or should not). If the pinot has excessive tannin, it is inherently unlikely it will ever come into balance. On the other hand, it is undeniable that a top pinot will gain both bouquet and complexity if given several years in the cellar, and that a few will be delicious when 10 or more years old. Likewise, the decision when to drink a pinot — involving the trade-off between the loss of fruit and the gain in complexity — is as personal and subjective a decision as it is for any other variety.

So I do present a table, not without misgivings, and as much to counter the implication that pinot noir is not a great wine as anything else.

pinot noir

region	quality producers	wines with special cellaring qualities
victoria		
Geelong	Prince Albert, Scotchmans Hill	Bannockburn
Gippsland	Nicholson River	Bass Phillip
Macedon/Sunbury	Bindi, Cleveland, Rochford	
Mornington Peninsula	Dromana Estate, Kings Creek, Massoni Main Creek, Main Ridge Estate, Moorooduc Estate, Port Phillip Estate, Willow Creek	Paringa Estate, Stoniers
North-East Victoria		Giaconda
Yarra Valley	de Bortoli, Domaine Chandon, Long Gully, St Huberts, Seville Estate, Yarra Burn, Yarra Ridge, Yarra Valley Hills, Yering Station	Coldstream Hills, Diamond Valley, Mount Mary, Tarrawarra, Yarra Yering, Yeringberg
south australia		
Adelaide Hills	Ashton Hills, Barratt, Grosset, Henschke	Lenswood Vineyards
western australia		
Lower Great Southern	Goundrey, Old Kent River, Plantagenet	Karriview, Wignalls
tasmania		
Northern Tasmania	Delamere, Heemskerk, Notley Gorge, Pipers Brook, Rochecombe	Rotherhythe
Southern Tasmania	Apsley Gorge, Craigow, Springvale, Wellington, Winstead	Freycinet, Elsewhere
canberra district		
Canberra District	Lark Hill	

Henschke Hill of Grace
The finite production from the 130-year-old
wines in the six-hectare vineyard means the price
of this great wine will inexorably continue to rise.

imported and
fortified wines

n a country such as Australia, with its own strong domestic production base, the export and import markets tend to be reverse sides of the same coin. A weak Australian dollar encourages exports and discourages imports; a strong dollar has the reverse effect. There is also a second effect: since 1984 — with a brief pause in 1989 — Australian wine exports have increased from 8.7 million litres to 165 million litres in late 1997 worth $645 million, with a genuine prospect of reaching $1 billion per annum by the year 2000. If nothing else, it should make us realise just how good (and how inexpensive) our wines are in world terms.

imported wines

Like any other normal, red-blooded Australian, I suffer both from the cultural cringe and no less from that knockdown sense of humour which betrays an underlying sense of discomfort in facing up to success. But I think that one has to be very perverse indeed not to recognise that, as young wines, Australia's rank with all but the very greatest (and infinitely more expensive) French wines. Take a 10- or 20-year perspective, however, and the picture is far less clear-cut. If there is a single general quality differentiation factor between Australian and French wines, it is the capacity of the latter to age with far more grace than our wines. If you take a classed-growth Bordeaux of one of the excellent recent vintages

('89, '90, '95 or '96) and compare it with one of our premium cabernets of similar age, little will be lost in the comparison as far as the Australian wine is concerned. However, take, say, 30 Bordeaux reds, 1970 vintage, and compare them with 30 Australian cabernets from 1970, and a very different picture will emerge. The quality of the Bordeaux reds will be remarkably consistent: some may be approaching their peak, some (depending on one's view of these matters) may even be at their peak, but quite certainly none will be past it. There will be a brilliance of colour, with absolutely no brown hues apparent; the bouquet will be bell clear and harmonious; while the palate will be beautifully balanced and long-lasting in terms of finish. You may be very lucky and have one or two Australian reds which answer that description, but the majority will not, and there will be enormous variation in quality, style and condition. You may well say that in Chapter 5 I have waxed lyrical over some great old Australian reds, and, in effect, mounted a case for medium- to long-term cellaring of the reds of today and tomorrow. It is true; I do so. But what I am saying here is that the rewards will be far less certain than in the case of the past great wines of Bordeaux.

I am a chronic disbeliever in vintage charts, and in any event there are ample books on the wines of Bordeaux, as well as constant reviews in specialist wine magazines of the cellaring prospects and potential of all of the great post–Second World War vintages. So it is with the greatest diffidence that I provide a bird's-eye (and highly personalised) view of the quality (and hence cellaring potential) of Bordeaux (and other European wines) since the 1987 vintage in Appendix 2. In summary, however, these are the cellaring specials of today's wine world.

Red burgundies are a far more chancy business than Bordeaux. Pinot noir is an intensely temperamental variety, and does well only when conditions favour it most. But choosing red burgundies is fraught with a second and even greater difficulty: one must have an encyclopaedic knowledge of the makers of burgundy, and one must never buy a burgundy without first having tasted it. Nor is it sufficient to taste a burgundy of a given commune of a given vintage and from a given maker, and assume that the other wines from the same maker and same vintage (but a different commune or different vineyard) will be of similar quality and style. It is quite certain that they will not be. So once again my view in Appendix 2 must be taken with the greatest possible caution.

Curiously, buying white burgundy is a far less dangerous pastime. Chardonnay seems to ride over the vicissitudes of vintage, and in the last 20-odd years only a handful of vintages have been abject failures across the board. Maker variation is still an important issue and, once again, anyone who buys a white burgundy without first tasting it deserves what he or she gets. But the broad style is far more consistent. The three issues to be determined are, firstly, do you prefer it to the far fruitier and up-front style of Australian and Californian chardonnays; secondly, are you prepared to accept the enormous price differential; and thirdly, do you have the patience to cellar the wines to allow them to realise their full potential? Having made the point ad nauseam that the 'when to drink' decision is a personal one, I nonetheless believe that to drink white burgundy (made in the traditional manner) when it is anything less than five years of age is a mortal sin.

My hardline views about drinking young white burgundy become yet harder when it comes to young sauternes. Here, I believe that with a few exceptions such as Chateau Rieussec, even to consider drinking sauternes younger than 10 years of age is to risk damnation of one's everlasting vinous soul. Young sauternes really are unpleasant: they are unbalanced, aggressive and unrewarding unless one has a hide (and a palate) of leather. From around 10 years of age, great sauternes start to shrug off the effects of the large additions of sulphur dioxide, the harsh phenols start to soften, and the wine blooms into a symphony of gold, honey and nectar. I suppose that I must also admit that exceptional vintages such as 1989 and 1990, and an increasingly evident change in French winemaking attitudes as the world moves away from the use of sulphur dioxide as a food (or wine) preservative, make me wonder whether my stricture will be so absolute in another 10 years. (Appendix 2 once again provides a guide to the more desirable vintages.)

rhône valley: rediscovered

My path across France now becomes a little more erratic. The random pin happens to impale the Rhône Valley, until the mid-1980s undervalued and a source of outstanding wine at a fraction of its true worth. However, America has discovered the Rhône Valley, and Jaboulet, Guigal, Clape, Jasmin, Chave and Reynaud are now revered in fine wine circles in America. Suffice it to say that the Rhône Valley provides a multitude of styles fashioned either from a single grape variety (syrah) at the northern end or from a bewildering array of up to 13 different varieties in a single blend at the southern end. The wines labelled Hermitage (which is also an *appellation controlée* district) and Côte Rôtie are the longest-lived. One hundred and thirty years ago they had a value equal to or in excess of the first-growth wines of Bordeaux, which were not above incorporating 10 per cent of syrah to bolster weak Bordeaux vintages and proudly advertising that fact on their label of the time. (Cabernet shiraz has a far more ancient and honourable history than most Australians realise.) It follows too that these great wines of the northern end can handsomely repay cellaring; anyone with 1961 Jaboulet Hermitage La Chapelle in their cellar is indeed thrice blessed. (Appendix 2 gives a summary view of the most recent vintages.)

From the Rhône Valley one travels north to the three remaining major French districts: Alsace, Champagne and the Loire Valley. I have already commented on the surprising longevity of Alsace riesling but, sadly, few readers of this book will have either the information or the opportunity to see for themselves, so I will pass on.

champagne: young or old?

Old champagne is a subject which provokes fierce debate: the Champenoise are past masters at promoting and selling their product, and this basically means current vintage wine (current in the sense of the most recently declared and shipped vintage) or current non-vintage stocks. The idea is that you buy it when it is ready to drink, drink it promptly, and then buy more. The Champenoise will privately admit to the extraordinary quality and virtue of very old vintage champagne which has been left on its lees in the cellars of the champagne house, and disgorged especially for honoured visitors from France or abroad. It is then traditionally disgorged no more than 24 hours before it is to be consumed. Over the years, I have had more than my fair share of such wonderful wines: '28 Krug, '21 Pol Roger, and '37 Salon remain indelibly imprinted on my memory. But these are curiosities, aberrations from the normal pattern — or, at least, that is how the Champenoise would have it.

On the other hand, there is a great tradition of cellaring champagne in England and, to a lesser degree, in America. Such wines, it must be said, progressively lose champagne character as the mousse subsides, and the wine moves closer and closer to table wine or, to be more precise, a rather unusual but very great old white burgundy. The gas may visually disappear from the bottle (and from the glass once the wine is poured), but the dissolved carbon dioxide acts as a preservative, and can still be felt as a faint prickle on the tongue. Thirty-, forty- or fifty-year-old champagnes drunk in this condition (in other words, disgorged decades earlier and privately cellared) are an easily acquired taste, although relatively few people have the opportunity of such an acquisition. The moral is, don't be afraid to try or, perhaps more relevantly, to buy the occasional old bottle of champagne which comes up for sale at auction. Because the virtues of such wines are so little appreciated, they often sell for little more than the price of the current vintage.

the loire valley: heavenly honeysuckle

Finally, there is the Loire Valley. At the eastern (or inland) end, sauvignon blanc reigns supreme. Do not cellar such wines; but if in a fit of enthusiasm you purchase too much of a young Sancerre or Pouilly Fumé, and still have some left five or six years later, you may have a pleasant surprise. But the odds are against it, and the gain in complexity barely compensates for the fruit loss in those wines which do stand the test of time. On the other hand, at the western or seaboard end of the Loire Valley, one comes across chenin blanc and some of the longest-lived white wines in the world: those of Vouvray and Anjou. I have 20 vintages of Marc Bredif Vouvrays going back to 1921 in my cellar, and have drunk a 1911 from the same maker. A little further south, one comes to Anjou and to the fabled cellars of Moulin Touchais. The reserves of Marc Bredif are no more, but until a few years ago dated back to 1874; Moulin Touchais goes back just as far, and in almost unbelievable quantity. These semi-sweet wines (the residual sugar is about the level of a German spatlese, but the weight of the wine is much greater) seem virtually ageless: the flavours range from honey to honeysuckle to marmalade to quince, but there is always a pleasant drying acid on the finish to balance the fore- and mid-palate sweetness. Bonnezeaux is another small appellation which makes wines of similar style; again, old vintages are still obtainable and, again, will amaze the uninitiated.

riesling: age is grace

Old German rieslings are little appreciated outside their home country, but can give great pleasure. Some years ago I secured a few bottles of 1887 and 1880 vintage Rheingau from Christie's: all but one of those bottles has opened in perfect condition, tasting more like a 20-year-old than a 100-year-old wine. In more recent memory, the 1921 vintage was outstanding, and the few trockenbeerenauslesen and beerenauslesen that have survived and that occasionally come onto the auction market deservedly bring very high prices. The great vintages of the last 40 years are 1959, 1964, 1971, 1976, 1983, 1990 and 1996; of these, probably the '76s should be drunk first (particularly on the basis that the older wines will be few and far between in any event). Basically, it is the spatlese and sweeter wines that should be cellared: the wine feeds off the residual sugar, and gradually dries out, but without becoming hard and empty. The older the wine, the easier it is to match with food.

Other wines of Europe which have exceptional cellaring potential include the exceedingly rare and expensive Hungarian tokay essence (survivors from the eighteenth and nineteenth centuries which come up at Christie's are among the highest priced wines to appear regularly in the auction market), and wines such as Italy's Brunello di Montalcino of Biondi Santi. Here one gets into ultraspecialised areas which are really beyond the scope of this book.

fortified wines

Then there are the fortified wines of the world, headed by vintage port. That ports are the longest-lived of all wines is a commonly held misconception: it is simply not so in the view of the port houses and of the at times eccentric but ever interesting families of expatriate Englishmen who have for generations owned and run the port houses. In 1983, when I visited Portugal during vintage and had lunch at the famous Factory House, their view was that the '66s were then going past their best; that the '63s were coming on far more rapidly than anyone had realised or anticipated, and would soon be ready to drink; and that the '70s were eminently ready.

Australia, too, makes some very distinctive and high-quality vintage port, very different in style to that of Portugal but superior to anything else outside of Portugal. Californian vintage ports, in particular, are to be avoided at all costs: they are vile concoctions that would be regarded as unsaleable in Australia.

In both Australian and Portuguese vintage port, a massive process of deposit takes place as the wine ages, with both tannin and tartrate encrusting the side of the bottle as it lies maturing. There is likewise a very marked colour change from the impenetrable purple-black of a very young port, to the glowing red of a port in its prime, and ultimately to a colour not very different from a tawny port with extreme age. Throughout this time, the raw, sweet and tannic fruit of the very young wine becomes lighter and lighter, and very often the ethereal lift of the spirit can become more evident.

Vintage port is, in fact, the only recognised style of fortified wine that improves in bottle. All other fortified wines (notably the sherry family, tawny ports, muscats and tokays) have been aged and developed in old oak barrels; once imprisoned in glass they enter a stage of suspended animation and, particularly in the case of sherries, will actually deteriorate in glass.

sherry: drink it, don't cellar it

That is certainly the case for fino and manzanilla, and in Spain such wines are drunk either direct from cask or from large demijohns with a very rapid turnover. If these wines are bottled, most producers would strongly recommend that the bottle be opened and drunk within three to six months of bottling.

I have to admit to a severe case of addiction to Manzanilla, that most delicate of all finos, magically produced by the sea breezes which blow through the lodges (or cellars) at Sanlucar de Barrameda. I regularly buy the wine in Australia (Hildago's La Gitana is my favourite, imported by the de Burgh-Day Wine Company) but always ensure it comes from a recently arrived shipment. Manzanilla and fino sherries are bottled with little or no sulphur dioxide, and come direct from a delicate balance in the cask between oxygen and the flor yeast growing on their surface.

Imprisoned in a bottle, they slowly lose that unique freshness and vitality. Likewise, once opened they should be refrigerated and consumed quickly — within days for a Manzanilla (or so I tell my wife).

The heavyweight sherries of the oloroso and cream style do not suffer so badly or so immediately from being bottled, and there is even a school of thought in England that supports the old-bottled style for olorosos. One suspects, however, this may be as much a matter of expediency as anything else, being a means of persuading would-be buyers of the virtues of unsold old-bottled styles. It is true that the deterioration would not be marked, and one would need to compare a freshly bottled sample of the same oloroso with one that had been in bottle for, say, two years to detect the difference.

All of this raises a fairly obvious question: why is it that one wine style (vintage port) improves in bottle, while all others are either unaffected by bottle-age or actually deteriorate? Vintage port is bottled early in its life, often within six or so months of vintage, and before it has started to polymerise the very high concentration of tannin, tartrate and raw anthocyanins. These processes will occur slowly in the bottle and, as they do, the vintage port will gradually lose the harshness of youth until at 10 to 30 years of age, depending on the power of the particular vintage, it develops the velvety sweetness of a mature vintage port.

In wood-matured fortified wines, these changes will take place in the barrels in which they are stored — changes which are accelerated where the oak container is of small size. Thus sherry and tawny ports (which spend a long time in oak) are all stored in small barrels which vary in size from 250 to 330 litres. Incidentally, new oak is not considered suitable for this task, and is usually 'seasoned' with a few vintages of inferior quality table wine before being used for fortified wine, and even then it is employed first for lesser grades of fortified wine. The object is not to pick up oak flavour, but simply to allow that process of controlled oxidation and polymerisation to take place; as the barrel ages, the deposits of tartrate grow ever thicker, and the pick-up of oak flavour ceases. Once the wine is bottled, these slow ageing processes (often accelerated by deliberately storing the barrels in the hottest part of the winery, ideally near a tin roof) are brought to an end.

Accordingly, while the complete cellar should have a cross-section of vintage ports of varying ages, it is not really necessary to lay down any of the other fortified wines in any quantity. In Australia, at least, most aficionados will nonetheless have a collection of old-bottled fortified wines, because they (rightly) feel that commercial pressures must sooner or later place unhappy strains on the stocks of very old tokay and muscat which are at the core of the highest quality releases of this style. The great makers such as Morris, Baileys and Chambers still have tiny blending stocks of extremely old (dating back to the last century) and concentrated blending material; as little as one per cent in a blend can have a substantial impact on the style and quality of the finished product.

Tyrrell's Vat 1 Semillon
On a par with McWilliam's Lovedale but, unlike Lovedale, made every year. This a brilliant example of the sheer magic in the bottle development of Hunter semillon over 10–20 years.

the cellar itself
cellar hardware

a cellar may be humble or grand, large or small. But if it is to qualify for the name, it must achieve three things. It should be dark, it should be free of vibration and, above all else, it should reduce both diurnal and seasonal temperature variation to a minimum. A cellar is not a series of ag pipes tastefully set into the wall of the kitchen, nor a wooden racking system sitting opposite the living room window adjacent to the central heating system. If such abominations must exist, they should be allowed to store wine for current use only: two weeks is an eternity in such vinous torture chambers.

The most difficult situation is that confronted by the flat-dweller, particularly if basement storage rooms are not available. As I indicate in Chapter 1, I solved the problem with warehouse storage, but then I had rather more bottles than most. So if one is limited to the flat, pride in display should take second place to practicality.

Inevitably, this will (or should) start with the wine carton and its interliners. Cardboard is a good insulator, as is newspaper, so leaving the wine in the carton is the first thing to do. If you have bought only one or two bottles of a particular wine, use a second-hand carton. If they are not to be drunk for a year or more, wrapping the bottles tightly in a few sheets of newspaper offers further protection against temperature variation (and, of course, light).

Obviously enough, any additional barrier against ambient temperature variation is useful. Cupboards are the most obvious, unless they are situated on an imperfectly insulated external wall which faces the afternoon sun. It all seems like commonsense, and usually it is, but there is always the unexpected. For a number of years my cellar was situated on the lower ground floor of a three-storey warehouse in the Sydney suburb of Pyrmont. The general warehouse area was cool and dark, and the space I occupied was walled off with a concrete ceiling for good measure. I took the lease in winter and happily moved into what I thought was the perfect cellar.

One warm spring day I visited, relaxing in the gloomy cool of the main warehouse area. But as I unlocked the door to the cellar, I was greeted by a rush of distinctly warm, indeed hot, air. Fire having been quickly discounted, I embarked on a journey of investigation to find that the concrete ceiling — which had always vaguely puzzled me — was the floor of the loading dock fronting on the back (and higher) street entrance. Although the concrete was very thick, the sun shone directly onto it throughout the late morning and early afternoon, and eventually heated the slab through.

I had no option: either the ceiling had to be insulated or air-conditioning installed. The ceiling had a maze of old and new fire sprinkler heads and pipes, so air-conditioning it had to be. And since the possibility of air-conditioning exists in virtually any cellar one can conceive, now is as good a time as any to explain its advantages and disadvantages. In turn these can be understood only when compared to the perfect cellar — which is to be found in the dungeons of a Scottish castle.

As I recounted earlier, one of the most fabulous collections of claret (I use the English terminology here, meaning Bordeaux reds, in this particular instance Chateau Lafite and Chateau Mouton-Rothschild) auctioned at Christie's in London came from Glamis Castle. The quantity of these wines, dating from the golden pre-phylloxera vintages of the 1860s and 1870s, was prodigious. But even more remarkable was the quality of the wines, typified by the abnormally small ullage in most of the bottles and magnums, none of which had been recorked. The secret lay in the year-round temperature of 8 degrees Celsius, and in the relatively high humidity of the Glamis cellars.

There are four components of ideal cellar conditions: an absolutely constant temperature, varying between neither day and night nor summer and winter; substantial humidity; a very cold mean temperature; and the absence of air movement (let alone any movement of the bottles). The first two factors are of major importance; the third is important but needs to be taken in context; while the last is of least importance.

Constancy of temperature is more important than the degree of temperature. Thus a cellar with a temperature varying between, say, 8 degrees Celsius and 13 degrees Celsius is inferior to a cellar with a consistent year-round temperature of, say, 15 degrees Celsius. Temperature variation is harmful because, as I have explained in Chapter 2, it leads to the expansion and contraction of the wine in the bottle, hastening the ingress of oxygen — and thereby oxidation.

Admittedly the extreme cold of the Scottish Highlands may be perfect for 100-year storage, but for an all-purpose cellar (which includes wines which you wish to mature rather than freeze into immobility) 8 degrees Celsius is excessively cool. Moreover, the additional cost of maintaining such a temperature (as opposed to a more conventional 16 to 18 degrees Celsius) is a significant deterrent.

Most conventional air-conditioners will not chill the temperature below 16 degrees in any event. This limitation accepted, the main drawback of conventional cooling is the dehumidification of the air. This may be excellent for preserving labels, but over time (even a year is sufficient) it will dry out the outer end of the cork. In the short term this results in the cork becoming brittle and tending to 'core out' as the corkscrew is withdrawn. In the very long term, the cork shrinks and dries to the point where it loses contact with the top section of the neck. The bottom section will remain moist because of its contact with the wine, but eventually it becomes an imperfect seal, losing its elasticity and ultimately crumbling.

So humidity is essential, ideally in the range of 70 to 75 per cent. There are, of course, sophisticated air-conditioning systems which incorporate humidifiers. Short of these, several large dishes (square plastic washing-up types are ideal) filled with water will help alleviate the problem.

Another disadvantage of air-conditioning is the forced air movement it necessarily induces. Ten years ago Seppelt built a very large, very functional and supremely boring Colorbond insulated warehouse at Great Western for storing its sparkling wines. Then and now the company also had almost two kilometres of old champagne drives carved in soft, decomposed granite by former goldminers employed by Joseph Best after the gold ran out in the 1870s and 1880s. One would have thought that these drives, with a temperature which does not vary below 12 degrees Celsius nor above 14 degrees Celsius would be perfection. But no; apart from that minuscule variation, almost imperceptible air currents moved naturally along the drives. So the totally stable and equally totally sterile shed was preferred. In the real world of the everyday cellar, such degrees of perfection are — obviously enough — largely irrelevant. But not totally irrelevant, for they at least point to the objectives one should have in establishing a home cellar.

The average suburban house, built on flat land during the past 20 years, is the next step up from a flat or unit. Walls will be thin (typically brick veneer or timber) and insulation will be minimal. And unless there is central air-conditioning, such a house is likely to provide an even less sympathetic environment than a flat or unit, and space will be at a similar premium. But it does offer two substantial advantages: foundations and a garden.

Over the years I formed a close acquaintance with the undersides of a variety of houses, both old and new. The longest, and most ambitious, attack was mounted on a small Federation-era house owned by a friend at Cammeray. It did not have formal access to under the house, but an inspection entrance was soon enlarged and my friend began the long process of jack hammering away the solid sandstone on which the house was built.

At first he and his friends (a passing parade, it must be said) worked on hands and knees, and at least the broken rock could easily be tipped out the doorway. But as the level fell, and aching backs straightened, so the doorway became ever higher and more distant. The rock had to be hauled out with a bosun's-chair-type device, which was almost as exhausting to use as the jackhammer. Finally, the great day arrived: the last touches were put to a marvellously cool, beautifully squared-off, finely chiselled sandstone cellar. But so did the first heavy rain for some months: the cellar immediately filled with water. Mercifully, the wine had not gone in, so all was not lost: a sump and a pump with a float switch were hastily installed. Nonetheless, power can fail (as can float switches), so a secondary record (also necessary for insurance purposes) of the contents of any cellar that can be flooded should be kept away from the cellar. Many low-lying cellars were caught in the Sydney floods of the 1980s; once labels float off, all one has is the capsule for identification and (with

Australian wines) occasionally branded corks indicating the producer and, rarely, the vintage.

In more modern houses, external access through the walls or footings to the space beneath the house may be impossible. Certainly, it is as well to check with a builder or architect before one's enthusiasm leads to ominous cracks in walls and ceilings. Cellars are a known cause of marital discontent, and an assault on the integrity of the house might well put the icing on the cake. If caution is recommended, or if your courage fails you, there is always the alternative of cutting a hole in the floor, making a trapdoor, and then excavating underneath the floorboards. I also have first-hand experience of this technique; my octogenarian parents had such a cellar, as does my brother. When covered by a carpet, it has the added advantage of being burglar-proof (unless it is an inside job). Here, memories of Second World War films featuring escapes from prisoner of war camps come readily to mind. Even when the back-breaking work is finished, space is usually limited, and one tends to emerge from the cellar looking like a caricature of Toulouse-Lautrec.

Finally, there are the grand or formal cellars. In old houses these can be readily fashioned out of the cavernous area which builders of the time seemed to favour, while in modern houses they can be purpose-built. But no matter what the origin of the cellar, be aware that in mainland Australia at least, there is a very significant difference between summer and winter temperatures. Any reasonably protected cellar will therefore feel warm in winter and cool in summer. This temperature differential from the outside ambient temperature is no doubt the cause of the proud boast, 'My cellar varies only one or two degrees year-round.' Unless that cellar is air-conditioned, the boast is an empty one, however genuinely the owner may believe in it.

One of the first things I did on building my first cellar (remember it was carved out of rock and effectively had a two-storey house on top) was to install a double-bulb thermometer. As well as providing the temperature at any given time, this type of thermometer also records the minimum and maximum reached. I threw away the magnet so as to avoid the temptation to remove the incriminatory evidence of minima and maxima. While the temperature never changed more than 1 degree in any 24-hour period, there was a 10 degree Celsius variation between mid-winter and mid-summer temperatures (or at least, the peak midwinter and peak mid-summer). This simply reflected the ambient temperature of the surrounding earth and rock slowly rising and falling with the change in season.

My present cellar (concrete floor, concrete roof, with a house on top of the roof, and double brick walls with styrene insulation between the two skins of bricks) seldom falls below 13 degrees, and equally rarely rises above 21 degrees, but once again the maximum/minimum thermometer destroys the illusion: the year-round variation is 8 degrees.

If marital or structural impediments prevent building a cellar anywhere in or under the house, there is always the back garden, and the specialist cellar-builders who operate in various parts of the world, Australia included, can do marvels with such a structure. Details of those companies who provide such services can be obtained from the building centres and home improvement centres that operate in each capital city.

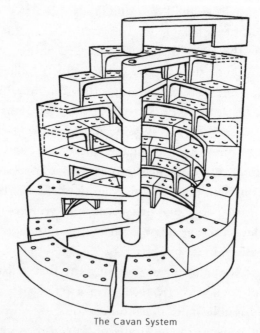

The Cavan System

One system available in Australia was developed in Europe, and is a prefabricated and patented design known as Cavan. It is an ingenious system in which precast concrete modules act simultaneously as stairs, walls and storage areas. Its limitation is that it does not permit single-bottle storage; the standard depth provides storage for 1500 bottles.

If your budget does not run to such luxuries, a commonly used do-it-yourself method is to sink a cement rainwater tank, access being provided by a spiral staircase installed in the centre of the tank.

cellar racking: cheap and simple or complex and costly

Wherever the cellar be, the next consideration will be the racking system. For the reasons I have discussed earlier, the wine carton has a number of advantages, chiefly turning on its insulation capacity. However, in Australia at least, almost all cartons are cardboard, and in the long or the short term (depending on humidity, water penetration and the like) are unsuitable to the point of being dangerous in most underground cellars. The great French wines are very often sold in wooden boxes, sometimes with the added protection of wood shavings or straw, and these are excellent storage media. The once ubiquitous but now rare Australian wooden banana or fruit box served the same function in a more rustic fashion.

Laid on their sides, the wooden boxes can be stacked three or four high, providing 'bulk' or 'bin' storage which is very cheap. The upmarket alternative is the purpose-built wooden diamond bin, with crosspieces each running at 45 degrees, and usually designed to take 12 bottles, but sometimes 18. Bulk storage of this kind is the cheapest and most space-economic, but also the least flexible. Either the bin is progressively emptied (thus losing its space economy) or it houses a jumble of different wines. If one wishes to get a wine from the middle or bottom, all of the other wines in the bin are disturbed, and repeated disturbance is no less inimical to long-term storage than is extreme temperature variation.

Recently, a box has come onto the market which may provide the answer for those who simply have no space for a normal cellar or who live in the hottest parts of Australia. Cellar Box, as it is called, is the brainchild of a Melbourne businessman, Tony Jackson, who has a small plastic foam-moulding business. He has designed and built a heavy-duty styrofoam box which holds a dozen bottles, and which can be stacked vertically or horizontally. Each box has a heavy-duty lid, and the insulation properties of the box when it is kept closed are very impressive. The system was put through a torture trial during a summer at Jackson's Collingwood factory. Over a five-week period, when the ambient temperature rose as high as 34 degrees in the factory, the temperature inside the Cellar Box (measured by a thermometer in a bottle of water in the Box) did not rise above 22 degrees, nor drop below 17 degrees.

There is then a host of open racking systems, all of which provide single-bottle storage but which have no insulation capacity. The permutations and combinations are endless. Some systems offer single-bottle storage, others bulk storage (that is, in lots of 12 to 14 bottles) while others provide a predetermined mix of bulk and individual storage. There is a range of unit sizes and a wide choice of construction materials ranging from metal to plastic-coated wire to wood. Some require little or no installation, others a degree of home-handyman expertise, while one or two need a professional to erect and install them. The choice will depend on the size of the cellar, the importance (or otherwise) of aesthetic appeal and, of course, on the extent of your budget.

The first decision to be made is whether you wish to have the convenience of single-bottle storage or the apparent space and cost economy of bulk storage. I say 'apparent' because experience shows that the bulk bins (which typically hold a dozen champagne bottles or 13 to 14 standard-sized bottles) usually have only a 60 per cent occupancy rate.

The reason is obvious enough: while the newly purchased dozen is happily accommodated, sooner or later you will start to drink the wine. The first bottle removed is barely noticed, and it is not until four or five have been taken out that you consider restocking. But what then? If you have gone for a mixed bulk bin and single-rack system, it is probable your single bottle storage is full up. If you fill up the bin with another wine, it becomes difficult to extract the wine in the bottom of the bin. So not until you have only three or four bottles left will the situation become truly manageable.

Some practical research has led to the conclusion that the best combination is 70 per cent individual bottle and 30 per cent bulk storage. This will presumably hold true for the larger and more serious cellar, in which dozen lots are likely to remain untouched for a year or more, but not for the smaller collection with a more rapid turnover. Here single-bottle storage will be at a premium.

Certainly, when I established my first permanent cellar I opted exclusively for single-bottle storage. But then I had ample room and, as I recount in Chapter 1, the wire beer crates I used cost only $1 each, or 8¢ per bottle. So, if space or money or both are real constraints, it is probable you will choose a mixed storage system, and equally probable that in the fullness of time you will wonder why you did so.

rack design: beauty or function?

The next decision is aesthetic. Is appearance very important? If so, do you prefer the solidity and the rather obvious presence of pine or the rather more discrete profile of most of the metal racking systems? The descriptions in Appendix 7 give you some idea of the choice involved, but you have in all probability seen the alternatives in wine shops or in friends' cellars. If not, it is best to do so before committing yourself.

Another consideration is whether you are going to establish the full racking system (whatever the type) in one go, or whether you are going to acquire and build it progressively. If the former, and your cellar is a substantial one, you should talk to several suppliers. Many are happy to provide custom-made installations and almost all will give a significant discount on bulk purchases of standard packs or modules.

So ultimately the choice comes down to a particular system and a particular supplier. The technical details given in Appendix 7 should give you most of what you need to come to a decision.

If all this seems too difficult, or if your house, flat or unit is simply unsuited to establishing a cellar, there are several specialist storage services available. Langton's itself offers storage facilities for its auction clients in Sydney and Melbourne, but rapidly filling space has led it to establish a strategic alliance with Millers Self Storage, which has recently begun a wine storage division.

In Sydney, for example, Millers has a refrigerated basement cellar maintained at 15 degrees Celsius and a humidity level of 65 per cent. Wine is stored by the case on racks or in a separate lock up space; both customers and cases are identified by barcode numbers. The addresses and phone and fax numbers of the four east coast locations are given in Appendix 7.

Yarra Yering Dry Red No 1
The idiosyncratic label reflects the great personality
of proprietor/winemaker Bailey Carrodus, but there
is nothing idiosyncratic about this long-lived
Bordeaux blend.

maintaining the cellar

In the previous chapter I have discussed the basic criteria for establishing a cellar (using that term to mean the room or physical surroundings housing the wine rather than the wine itself). In this chapter I look at the housekeeping aspects of maintaining the cellar — both its physical structure and the wines placed in it. I will assume that you have done the best you can in this regard to create adequate cellar conditions (particularly avoiding rapid temperature fluctuations) and that now we are looking at the day-to-day and year-to-year housekeeping chores that can and will arise.

In all except the model cellar, control of humidity can be a problem. I have dealt with the drying effects of conventional air-conditioning, and suggested ways of returning moisture to the air. However, particularly in the more humid parts of Australia (in Sydney and Brisbane, and of course along the northern coastline), excess humidity can be a real problem. In the warm summer months, moulds can grow at a feverish pace, completely destroying labels or staining them to the point where they can barely be deciphered, or dissolving the glue which holds the labels onto the bottles (or all three).

This was a major problem in the cellar I once had at Turramurra in Sydney's northern suburbs, but I found that if I placed a small household fan at either end of the cellar set on low speed, the gentle air movement was sufficient to control mould growth. Do not, however, place the fans so that they blow directly onto the bottles; do not have them oscillating; and do not set them on high speed. The object is to create a gentle air movement, and to avoid forcing an irregular draft directly onto the bottles.

Turning to the other side of the coin, and to excessively dry conditions, another method of humidity control is to cover the floor with a fine screening of clean gravel. This certainly makes for a rustic feel, but also has the practical advantage that it can be watered with a watering can at weekly intervals to provide the appropriate moisture.

If the air in the cellar has insufficient moisture, the corks will progressively dry out from the outer end. The effect of this is manifested in one of two ways: most commonly, and in the shorter term, the centre of the cork will 'core-out' as the corkscrew is withdrawn. In other words, you will simply hollow out the cork, leaving the sides adhering to the bottle, and a terrible mess in the wine.

Under extremely dry and prolonged conditions of storage, the exposed end of the cork will actually weather and shrink, taking on the appearance of the bark of the tree it originally came from. I have acquired bottles with corks in this condition from Christie's auctions in London, although the wine itself was none the worse for the experience when opened. In the very long term, of course, one will be left with only a minimum length of viable cork (moistened from the wine at the bottom or business end) which will be dislodged by the slightest movement.

wine: best kept in the dark

When no-one is in the cellar, it should be kept in pitch darkness. Because the local council refused to believe that the cellar at my Turramurra home could indeed be simply that, and because it was convinced it would be used as a rumpus room, it insisted on a window being installed at the one point of the cellar which was above the ground. This light source was quickly dealt with by blackboard paint and, because it was a very small window which never received direct sunlight, it was not necessary to take the process one step further by affixing sisalation.

Fluorescent or other forms of electric light have little or no effect over short, intermittent periods. The effect is quite unlike that of heat over similarly short or intermittent periods, for example. On the other hand, light-bodied white wines and champagnes are far more sensitive to light than are red wines, and special care should be taken to protect these. Much research has been done in recent years on the effect of ultraviolet light on champagne, resulting in the malady called *goût de lumière*. It is now understood that ultraviolet light can in certain circumstances lead to the creation of hydrogen sulphide in champagne. The result is off-odours and tastes associated variously with cabbage and rotten eggs.

It follows from all this that the serious cellar should be just that: a cellar. It should not be a general entertaining or show-off area for large numbers of people to congregate in. Firstly, the very presence of a dozen or so guests will significantly increase the ambient air temperature; and secondly, the temptation to pick up and fondle the prized bottles of the cellar is almost irresistible. On the other hand, the presence of the proprietor alone has a markedly soothing effect both on the proprietor and, so I am prepared to believe, the wines.

denizens of the cellar: rats, cork moths and silverfish

A large cellar (of, say, more than 200 bottles) should be inspected carefully at least once a month, as nature is equipped with a disconcerting battery of vandals. Some years ago I returned from a week-long visit interstate to find mayhem had been inflicted on some of my oldest wines: a rat had found its way into the cellar, and had proceeded to chew through the oldest lead capsules, evidently seeking the glue and/or minute residues of dried wine for food. There was no damage to the wine itself, but the appearance of many old treasures was irrevocably impaired. That rat met its maker, but its brother returned to wreak the ultimate revenge — the destruction of several bottles of 1918 Chateau Coutet, achieved by pushing in the corks with its snout.

The cork moth is a more commonly encountered pest which can threaten an entire cellar. Over the years, several major Australian wine companies have been subject to infestation. The wines they sold were breeding grounds, and even a single bottle could prove a source of infection for an entire cellar. The cork moth is like any other moth; it has a grub-larvae-moth cycle. Its presence is usually indicated by fine, wispy strands of excrete hanging from the end of the bottle, just like that of a wood-borer. Small borer-like holes may be seen in the corks if the capsules are removed. The rats were ultimately dealt with by a rat trap, but cork moths are less easy to dispose of. One has to wait for the winged stage, and then hang pest-strips throughout the cellar. If the moth's life cycle is a mystery, then the only answer is to hang pest-strips permanently until all signs of activity cease.

Wine stored in cardboard cartons is subject to silverfish activity. One might think that the silverfish would confine their attentions to the cardboard containers, but quite evidently the labels offer a change of diet. The common chemical methods (insect sprays, and so on) usually bring a speedy end to such an invasion once it is noticed.

ullage: the unseen foe

But by far the most important housekeeping chore is keeping a watch on the condition of the corks as far as ullage is concerned. I have briefly outlined in Chapter 2 the significance of ullage and the adverse effects that excessive airspace in the bottle has on the wine. The loss of wine (or the build-up of ullage, for these are simply two sides of the one coin) may be very slow or relatively rapid. If the latter be the case, there will almost certainly be physical signs in the form of partly congealed, sticky, dark brown wine exuding through the capsule if the capsule has little round air holes cut in it. If the capsule is of solid lead, without these minuscule vents, the wine will be trapped inside. It may then corrode through the capsule or, in extreme cases, cause a minor swelling. One has to be eagle-eyed and become very expert to notice these signs. Nonetheless, the advantage of this level of inspection is that it does not require the bottle to be pulled from the rack and brought to the vertical position to assess whether or not there is a problem.

So the first process in checking ullage is one of elimination: if all appears well, a bottle-by-bottle inspection will not be necessary, nor the attendant disturbance of the wine. Instead, all that one should do every six or 12 months is remove one bottle in 12 of a given wine and, if there has been no marked change, it is reasonable to assume the other bottles will be in similar condition.

Alternatively, the ullage may develop very slowly. In this case, there will be no physical signs on the cork, and only an examination of the bottle will tell the story. One of the unknowns is the volume of the airspace left at the time the wine was bottled. The great wines of France characteristically have an air space of five millimetres or less at bottling. In

Australia, however, modern bottling lines which first of all sparge the empty bottle with inert gas, and then fill the bottle leaving a vacuum in the airspace (in other words, there is no oxygen present), often have a far greater airspace. The volume of that airspace will in fact correlate precisely to the contents of the bottle: the major wine companies are loath to give even an extra millilitre beyond the statutorily required 750 millilitres.

to recork or not to recork?

Since those selfsame companies also have a tendency to use the cheapest (and hence the shortest) corks possible, the airspace might be substantial. However, it should never result in the wine being less than five millimetres above the base of the neck, where the shoulder of the bottle commences to sweep out. And once the wine drops to the bottom of the neck, the alarm bells should start to ring. If the level has receded to this point while the wine is still relatively young (say 10 years or so) and you wish to cellar it for a further 10 years, quite obviously it should be promptly recorked. On the other hand, if you have a 50-year-old bottle of wine in your cellar, and the level is still at the base of the neck (or at the top of the shoulder), one would not dream of recorking it unless the wine is to be held for one's grandchildren. For while there may be no option but to recork, it is very much a question of choosing the lesser of two evils. There is inevitably an infusion of fresh oxygen, and inevitably the ageing process will be momentarily accelerated. The trade-off, though, is a slowing of that ageing process over the longer term once the recorking has been safely accomplished.

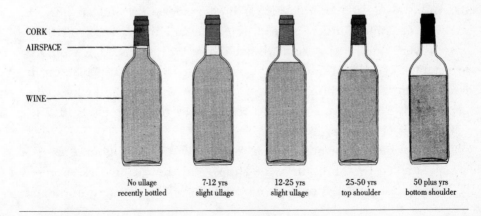

CORK
AIRSPACE

WINE

| No ullage recently bottled | 7-12 yrs slight ullage | 12-25 yrs slight ullage | 25-50 yrs top shoulder | 50 plus yrs bottom shoulder |

the technique of recorking

Once the decision to recork has been taken, there are two different basic scenarios: one is the recorking of a single, ancient and treasured bottle; the other is the recorking of a number of bottles of the same wine. Dealing with the latter, a bottle with typical ullage should be uncorked first. It should be tasted to ensure it is sound. If the wine is mouldy, oxidised or volatile it should immediately be discarded, and a second bottle opened. If that is in the same condition, you obviously have a problem and — depending on your conscience — the solution is either the auction room or the kitchen sink (or possibly the stockpot).

If, however, the first or second bottle opened is in sound condition, it should be used as the topping-up bottle. In other words, the next bottle should be uncorked (gently, so as to cause the minimum disturbance to the contents), being kept in a vertical position at all times. It need not be tasted, but simply topped up immediately to a level three millimetres below the cork, and recorked immediately.

Astute readers will realise I have taken several things for granted so far. First, one should experiment with the corking machine and the chosen corks by taking an empty bottle of the same shape as that of the bottles to be recorked, to establish precisely where the bottom end of the cork will finish once it is inserted. A felt-pen mark should then be made on the empty bottle the appropriate distance below the cork, and this becomes the measuring stick for the bottles to be recorked.

The other missing links are the corks and the corking machine. Both may be obtained from the home winemaking shops that exist in all of the major capital cities. The more expensive the wine being recorked, the more essential it is to procure high-grade corks and an efficient corking machine. This, of course, is easier said than done, and if the wine is very rare or you count yourself very inexperienced, it would be preferable to seek professional aid from a winemaker or a specialist wine retailer who deals in bulk wine. Of course, if you are the lucky owner of Penfolds Grange, you can have recourse to the Penfolds Red Wine Clinics described on page 12.

Corks come in various grades; regrettably, the best grades are not always stocked by the home wine shops, and the major cork suppliers are simply not prepared to deal in quantities of less than one thousand.

Nonetheless, if the wine is worth the trouble, it is worth the best corks you can purchase.

Corks obtained in bulk from cork suppliers usually come vacuum-packed and specially treated. The treatment not only sterilises active cork moulds but enhances the cork to glass seal and later promotes easier extraction of the cork. In a separate treatment process, they will have been coated with silicon to facilitate entry into the bottle. If you are buying corks from a home bottling shop, it would be wise to find out how old they are and, if possible, to insist on corks from a recently opened bag; it may also be useful to enquire whether they have been silicon-treated. (If the bag has been open for a long time the corks will no longer be wine sterile and their moisture content will be affected: this will ultimately affect the performance of the cork.)

Whatever the answers to those questions, you may still have difficulty with a hand-corking machine in persuading the cork to go readily into the neck of the bottle. Once again, you should practise on an empty bottle before recorking commences. If the corks refuse to go in at all, or if they are particularly difficult, they should be soaked for 30 minutes in warm water with one gram per litre of sodium metabisulphite added to the water as a sterilising agent. A dozen corks at a time should then be removed from the warm water bath and dried; the ideal method is to use a salad drier (if you have one). If not, simply shake them vigorously in a large plastic colander. If the recorking proceeds for any great length of time, the water should be changed (and re-sulphured) regularly.

A final complication of cork selection comes with the varying bottle neck sizes. Australians, as well as driving on the wrong side of the road so far as the French are concerned, have also resolutely refused to embrace wholeheartedly international standards for internal neck diameters. At this point the whole corking exercise really becomes too complicated and too technical: so the middle road is to purchase corks with a 24-millimetre diameter (the alternatives being 23 or 25 millimetres). Obviously, under certain combinations of cork and neck sizes, you may end up with a square peg in a round hole.

Then there is the question of the corker. Carefully look at the cork inserted in the empty bottle. Rotate the bottle under a strong light; a seam or line down the side of the cork may be apparent at one point. If it is apparent, you have a problem with the corker. The extent of that problem, however, can be determined only by inserting a cork in a bottle of red wine, leaving it upright for four hours, and then lying it on its side for 48 hours. If at the end of this period a telltale line of red has crept along the entire length of the seam, the cure of recorking may be worse than the illness.

The small, totally hand-held corkers (that is, corkers without a stand) are the worst offenders. The hand-operated but stand-mounted corkers, which have a variety of mechanisms for compressing the cork before it has entered in the bottle, are much better. They not only make far lighter work of the job, but — depending on the model and state of repair — may avoid the creasing or seaming problem altogether. In all of these matters, the presence of an expert (a real expert, that is) is invaluable.

Equipment assembled and technical problems all overcome, the recorking can proceed. The sequence here is to open a bottle to be recorked, top it up, and then immediately recork it, before withdrawing the cork from the next bottle. In this way the time the recorked bottles are opened to the air will be restricted to a matter of seconds. Even here, some prior preparation may be needed to have the system running at its most efficient: the old capsules should be removed from all of the wine to be rebottled, and the top of the bottle around the cork area scrupulously cleaned — either a stiff toothbrush or a coarse stainless steel wool pad (or a combination of both) does the best job.

Once the wine has been recorked, it should be allowed to stand up for a minimum of four hours (and preferably 24 hours) to allow the cork to swell out before the wine is laid on its side. Any recapsuling should be done at the same time as the recorking so that, once the wine is restored to its former position in the cellar, no further disturbance will be necessary.

capsules: largely ornamental

Incidentally, recapsuling is largely an ornamental process and for this reason alone can be regarded as an optional extra. What is more, it is extremely unlikely that you will be able to duplicate the original capsules and, unless you have access to a Knirps (or similar) capsuling machine, will not be able to apply the tin (previously lead) capsules which are used on premium-quality wines. If you have access to such a machine, its supplier will, of course, tell you how to use it. If you do not, there are a range of plastic push-on capsules (some requiring shrink-application) available at home winemaking shops. Once again, precise directions will come with the particular capsule chosen.

What if you have only one bottle to recork? What then do you top up with? Simply to replace the cork without replenishing the ullage would do more harm than good in most instances, so in these circumstances you have a choice: either select a second bottle of a similarly aged and styled wine, top up from it and drink the remainder of it, or simply use a younger wine made from the same grape variety or varieties. The latter practice is euphemistically known as 'refreshing' in France; it is not unknown for less than scrupulous proprietors to top up old wines in quantities using a deliberate infusion of very young wine to add that extra touch of fruit. It may be no bad thing for the wine, and only you will know about it, but of course you cannot fool yourself.

Under the most clinical and professional of circumstances, the whole process may be accomplished under cover of inert gas. However, those able to achieve this will have no need of this book, and so I shall not describe the means by which this can be achieved in the home cellar. It may, however, suggest to you the best possible way to have wines recorked: persuade your friendly winemaker to do so when next he or she is bottling some of his or her own wine.

cellar records: books or computers?

Then comes the question of stock control. There are many reasons why it is wise to keep a cellar book and, indeed, why one should keep more than one copy (or back up your computer). The first and most obvious is a record for insurance purposes in the event of burglary or fire. Certainly in the case of fire, and possibly in the case of burglary, the second record (kept at a separate place, even if not completely up to date) is an obvious precaution.

Cellar books come in all shapes and sizes. Sometimes they serve as a simple record of contents; sometimes they may incorporate details of purchase date and cost, as well as progressive usage; while the most elaborate form will also incorporate tasting notes. The cellar book may be just that, a bound volume; or it may be a loose-leaf volume; or it may turn on a card index system.

In this day and age of personal computers and word processors, the self-created cellar list is rapidly becoming the norm. Its configuration, and the amount of detail included, is strictly up to the author. The ordering of the contents may follow that of the cellar; alternatively, it may be arranged alphabetically within country of origin or within region. It goes without saying that basic computer programs can be written which will enable the computer user to rearrange the cellar and call up selections at will. Thus you can command a print-out of every 1986 vintage wine in the cellar, be it white or red, Australian or imported. Or you can call up every riesling or every riesling from 1990 — the permutations and combinations will be limited only by the imagination used in creating the program in the first place. A full cellar interactive program is contained in the CD ROM version of my *Companion to Australian and New Zealand Wine*.

WINE	Penfolds Grange Hermitage - 1980 Vintage
PURCHASED	November 1985 from Farmer Bros - $39.99

Location	Opening Stock	Used	Date	TASTING NOTES/COMMENTS
W12	12	1	2/2/86	Dark opaque red; immense concentration + power; very high tannins; nowhere near ready; great wine in the making.
W12	11	1	17/8/88	Only slight colour change; some gamey characters on bouquet; palate showing first signs of softening, but needs another 5 yrs.

cellar layout

Finally, there is the question of the physical organisation of the bottles within the cellar. There are no hard and fast rules. The system chosen will reflect the number of bottles in the cellar, the flexibility (or otherwise) accorded by the racking system chosen, the total space available, the range of wine types included and, lastly — and most importantly — the personal whim of the owner of the cellar.

If the cellar is a large one, featuring a comprehensive selection of the major wines of the world, it seems logical to break it up initially into white wines and red wines. Having done that, the white wines are first grouped according to country of origin and thereafter (if applicable) by variety. That is a system that would work well for France at least.

If the cellar is purely Australian or Australian-dominated, the white wine and red wine distinction is still a logical starting point, but it is then far more likely that the sub-groupings will be by region or, possibly, by maker. The point is, of course, that most Australian winemakers produce a wide range of white and red wine styles, whereas in France the range (by individual maker) is extremely limited, varieties and regions being largely pre-determined.

Having determined the basic organisation strategy, the next thing to deal with is bin numbers and (on individual bottle storage systems) bottle numbers. Once again, the necessity will vary according to the size of the cellar. If it is a large cellar and there are many single bottles or multiple vintages of a particular wine, it obviously helps to have a master list cross-referenced to the precise location of the wine in the cellar. Simply by way of example, I give the numbering system I employ in my own cellar. I have 40 or so of the ARC Weldmesh racks which I describe in Appendix 7. (I hasten to add that not all hold 720 bottles; some have been cut down to half size.) Each rack constitutes a module and has been given a letter identification running sequentially around the walls and cross-floor sections of the cellar. Having run through the letters from A to Z, I then recommence with AA, BB, and so on. Each vertical row of bottle-holes is given a number from 1 to 36 (or a lesser number in the case of a cut-down rack). The wines are arranged in vertical rows, and my cellar list then shows the rack number and the row number for a particular wine. Thus typically identifications would be B21, CC4, and so on. Certainly, the row may hold more than one type of wine, but it takes only a few seconds to locate the bottle in the row.

If your cellar is underground and there is the least possibility of flooding, precise identification of the location of the bottle becomes an important issue. Many proud owners have been left lamenting when floods have washed labels off bottles, making identification all but impossible. A separate record kept elsewhere is invaluable in this circumstance, and is almost always required by insurance companies in any event.

Giaconda 1991 chardonnay

grown in gravel-clay soil in the foothills of the victorian alps

13.3% a/v wine of australia 750 ml preservative 220 added

giaconda vineyard m°clay rd. beechworth vic.

Giaconda Chardonnay

This is the most scarce of the boutique chardonnays. It is crafted with fanatical care by Rick Kinzbrunner from a single hectare of vineyard, and ages with particular grace.

chapter nine

wine as an investment

i can honestly say that I have never acquired a single bottle of wine as an investment. Each and every bottle in my cellar was purchased with the intention of drinking it. I see no reason to suppose that my motivation over the next 20 years will be any different to that of the past 40 years.

Thus I have every sympathy for the views of Baron Elie de Rothschild. In the early 1970s, during one of the intermittent price booms in Bordeaux (and which preceded the horrendous crash of 1975) the Baron commented: 'The day I saw in Time magazine a photograph of a bank vault with a bottle of Lafite in it I assembled my staff and told them, "The crisis has started". Indeed, from the moment when you start to think of wine as an investment and not as something to be drunk, that's the end.'

Yet I would need to live to be 100, never buy another bottle of wine in my life, and drink a bottle every day if I were to have any hope of drinking all the wine I currently have in my cellar. What is more, over the years I have sold significant quantities of wine. Whether one cares to admit it or not, wine is a commodity that is regularly traded; in the world scene it suffers from the same extreme fluctuations in price as other commodities and, at least in one sense, it is — for better or worse — an investment.

boom and bust: the nineteenth century

The history of boom and bust is an ancient and honourable one. It is told in great detail and with great verve by Nicholas Faith in *The Wine Masters*

(Hamish Hamilton, 1978). Faith records that the period of the 1850s and 1860s was one of speculative investment of a dimension not to be encountered again for 120 years. The average price of Chateau Latour in the years 1854 to 1858 (modest vintages) was two and a half times the average of that for the previous 10 years. In the next few years, exports rose in leaps and bounds: spurred by a free-trade agreement concluded between England and France in 1860, exports to Britain doubled in 1860, and quickly rose to five times the 1859 levels. Prices were similarly volatile: the celebrated 1865 vintage doubled in price in a period of two years, and the wines of Bordeaux reached levels which in real terms were not to be approached again for over 100 years. It is hardly surprising that over 25 per cent of the classed-growth Chateaux changed hands during the period from 1850 to 1870.

Within years, the whole of Europe was caught in a major economic recession; it so happened that this coincided with the arrival of phylloxera in Bordeaux, and phylloxera has often been portrayed as the cause of the progressive decline in wine prices over the last 30 years of the nineteenth century. A little bit of logic would suggest that phylloxera (by savagely reducing output) should have led to an increase rather than a decrease in prices. The reality was otherwise: prices had risen too far and too quickly, and must have been subject to correction in any event. The general economic downturn simply acted as a multiplier to the collapse in prices.

boom and bust continued: the twentieth century

Worse was to follow. The First World War brought a brief period of speculation and rapid price rises between 1916 and 1919 not far short of those of the 1860s, but there was an equally precipitous and savage decline between 1920 and 1921. Prohibition in the United States and the hyperinflation in the German economy were among the contributing factors. A modest recovery was then followed by a rapid realignment of the English and French currencies, which saw the value of the pound sterling halved and made the 1926 vintage the most expensive in history for English buyers.

Then came the Great Depression and, with it, total misery. The price of a share in Chateau Latour fell from 28 000 francs in 1929 to 8000 francs in 1933. More significantly, the American banker Clarence Dillon was able to buy Chateau Haut-Brion in 1936 for the equivalent of A$250 000. Chateau Latour would have been sold had it not been for the realisation that it would fetch a derisory price.

The years following the Second World War produced a never-to-be-repeated string of vintages: '45, '47, '48 and '49 rank among the all-time great years, while 1950 produced some very pleasant and basically under-appreciated wines. But prices were to recover very slowly, so that when Christie's recommenced their wine auctions in 1966, it was possible to buy a case of 1945 Chateau d'Yquem for a mere £45 sterling. Even the small but superlative 1961 vintage did not cause a stampede. The turning point came with the '69, '70 and '71 vintages. Prices rose in leaps and bounds to the point where the '71 vintage of Chateau Latour provided sales revenue nine times greater than that received for the '55 vintage, one of Latour's finest.

In 1971 it was still possible to say that all that had happened was that the Bordelaise had finally caught up on a century of inadequate returns, and that the prices prevailing that year, while high, did no more than represent a fair return for great wine. The same could not be said for the madness of 1972, which was an appalling vintage in terms of quality but which brought prices far in excess of the great vintages of '61, 66 and '70. As first the Americans and then the Japanese clamoured for the wine, prices increased even more abruptly in the early part of 1973. Schemes abounded: everyone had a syndicate, and so great was the confidence that it was possible to insure the purchase price against any diminution in value for a premium of only one per cent.

the cruse scandal and the collapse of the market

Those who took out insurance were wise indeed. The end came with terrifying suddenness, prompted by three things: the oil crisis, an exceptionally prolific but mediocre 1973 vintage, and the breaking of the Cruse scandal.

The Cruse family was one of the most influential and highly respected members of the Bordeaux wine trade. The family owned a very large distribution business and also Chateau Pontet-Canet, the largest estate in Pauillac. In a celebrated trial various members were convicted of wine fraud in passing off inferior wine with false certificates of origin, and one of the Cruses leapt to his death from a bridge over the Gironde.

Demand for Bordeaux, which had previously seemed insatiable, dried up overnight. The stock markets of the world fell to all-time lows in 1974, and confidence in the British pound (remember that London has always been the wine-window of the world) evaporated.

In 1975 the Australian dollar was 1.30 or less to the pound, a figure at which I believe I purchased the bank drafts to pay for my purchases at Christie's auctions throughout that year. On 6 June 1975, the unthinkable happened: the two great contestants of the first growths, Chateau Lafite and Chateau Mouton-Rothschild, who had waged an unremitting battle for recognition as first amongst firsts, joined together to offer a huge volume of surplus stocks through Christie's.

from bust to boom

The contrast between 1975 and 1997 could not be greater: from dark depression to a boom of hitherto unimaginable proportions. Before I give a few examples of the extent of the changes in the value of the classic wines, let me briefly sketch in the intervening years. The bottom or trend line has been a continuous increase in prices, sometimes slowing, sometimes accelerating.

Between 1976 and 1983 the rate of increase was relatively slow: other than 1978, the vintages were unexciting, and there was a minor recession in 1983. But then Robert Parker burst on the scene with his rapturous reviews of the 1982 Bordeaux vintage (in April 1983), and those wines started to be shipped at the end of 1984. This coincided with a period of extreme weakness in the French franc, so even though ex-chateau prices were rising, the landed cost of French wine into Australia and the United States was very attractive.

A period of extreme activity followed until 1987/88, buoyed by a continuing run of very good to great vintages: '83, '85, '86, '88, '89 and '90. The first slowing came with the strong recovery of the franc, which magnified the effect of price rises ex-chateau. Then came the stock market crash of October 1987, followed in due course by a very deep and prolonged Australian recession (and a severe recession elsewhere).

Had it not been for that fabulous run of vintages, with each of '88, '89 and '90 proving even better than its predecessor, the story might have been very different. But as it was, prices continued to rise even in the face of the recession, doubtless because of the quality of the wines.

Three great vintages were followed by four very ordinary ones ('91 to '94 inclusive) in Bordeaux, though the '92 White Burgundies and '93 Red Burgundies were lights in the vintage gloom. The Bordeaux vintages operated to keep the market under some semblance of control until mid-1996, when the first *en primeur* offerings of the very good 1995 wines were made.

It quickly became apparent that a number of forces were at work. Initially, the traditional major markets in the United States and the United Kingdom simply reacted with pleasure to the arrival of an unequivocally good (though not necessarily great) vintage. But it also became clear that those markets had come out of recession with a powerful thirst and masses of money to spend. If this were not enough, powerful new markets developed with astonishing rapidity as Asian buyers returned with even greater eagerness than they exhibited back in 1972/73.

Staid English wine merchants shook their heads in disbelief at the spiralling prices of the 1995 Bordeaux, but a year later (in 1997) the 1996 *en primeur* price rises made the events of the previous year pale into insignificance. Having opened at 300 francs a bottle (70 francs more than the '95 opening prices), the first growth clarets from 1996 rose first to 500 francs with the second offering (or tranche), and closed at 700 francs with the final tranche. But during the 1997 VinExpo in Bordeaux in June 1997, prices as high as 1200 francs a bottle were being sought in the secondary (*negociant*) market. When delivered in Australia late in 1999, this would result in a retail price in excess of $600 per bottle.

Yet, as I recounted in Chapter 4, even these prices pale into insignificance compared to the activity in the London auction rooms in 1997. First came the Sotheby's sale of part of Lord Andrew Lloyd Webber's wine cellar in May 1997, a sale which raised £3.7 million and appeared to set new benchmarks. But more was to come with the Christie's two-day sale in September 1997 of part of an undisclosed vendor's (widely believed to be Hardy Rodenstock, a noted German collector) cellar which brought £8 million. And so I come to the promised examples of the shift in

Christie's auction prices between 1975 (for effect the lowest price paid in 1975 at auction) and its September 1997 auction. The prices are per case of one dozen bottles, in pounds sterling. To gain a true comparison, the buyer's commission of 10 per cent (not charged back in 1975) should be added to the 1997 prices.

Chateau Mouton-Rothschild

Auction Date	Vintage '45	Vintage '49	Vintage '61	Vintage '70
1975	280	210	180	62
1997	43 000	6000	8500	4200

Chateau Latour

Auction Date	Vintage '45	Vintage '49	Vintage '61	Vintage '70
1975	260	155	155	74
1997	14 400	14 000	13 000	1250

If you feel this is an unduly long time-frame, here are some comparisons between 1989 and 1997 prices (again in pounds sterling per case).

Auction Date	1982 Ch. Petrus	1982 Ch. Latour	1961 Hermitage La Chapelle
1989	2000	500	1260
1997	16 000	3800	19 000

Christie's has disclosed that 40 per cent of the wine purchased at the September 1997 sale went to Asian buyers, 32 per cent to Europeans, 11 per cent to Americans and 15 per cent to Canadians. Included in the European category was a substantial Moscow-based component: so it is that half of the wine went to markets that only a few years previously did not exist.

from boom to ?

Only time will tell whether there has been a fundamental and permanent change in both the geographical markets for and in the baseline prices of the great wines of France, or whether these are unreal and unsustainable prices.

In the short term, at least, it seems unlikely the price for either Champagne or Burgundy will follow Bordeaux's mad path. But if the prices do prove to be enduring, it will only be a question of time before the rest of France falls into line, with the Italians in hot pursuit.

There are also profound implications for the price of Australian wine, which in the wake of growth in exports since 1985 became an international commodity with international benchmark pricing. During the period from the end of 1995 to the end of 1997, some of the implications had already become apparent, with substantial, broad-based rises in the prices of premium bottle wine and, in particular, red wine.

The leader was, of course, Penfolds Grange. The following table of prices covering the wines released since 1990, using theoretical retail prices taken from Thomson's Liquor Guide, tells only part of the tale until you look at the last column which lists the retail prices for the same wines being offered by Vintage Cellars in 1997.

Vintage	Year of Release	Retail Price on Release	Retail Price 1997
1984	1990	57.75	265
1985	1991	68.00	265
1986	1992	74.25	445
1987	1993	84.00	247
1988	1993	92.60	247
1989	1994	100.00	220
1990	1995	127.50	445
1991	1996	144.20	310
1992	1997	166.59	300

The table is interesting for a number of reasons. First, it shows that, at long last, vintages are understood to be of importance in Australia — some excellent, some not. More important, however, is the trebling in the retail price of Grange in seven years; and yet, notwithstanding that increase, the huge profits available since 1995 for those able to procure Grange at 'normal' retail price (calculated with a mark-up of 35 per cent on the landed unit cost to the retailer), let alone those retailers, restaurateurs and so forth able to acquire it at wholesale cost from Penfolds.

the grange slipstream

The ground-breaking work of Grange led to a slipstream effect: Henschke Hill of Grace followed in the wake of Grange, its price trebling in as many years, in turn pulling Mount Edelstone along. Within the Southcorp group, the other super-premium red wines — most obviously Penfolds Bin 707 Cabernet Sauvignon, Wynns John Riddoch Cabernet Sauvignon, Wynns Michael Hermitage and Penfolds Magill Estate — likewise followed suit.

Behind these icon wines the entire premium and super-premium red wine market surged in price, yet demand remained unimpaired. The majority of Australia's best red wines were on more or less permanent allocation in 1997, with a tug of war between the competing demands of the domestic and export markets.

While the demand for premium bottled white wine was in better balance with supply, prices again rose, albeit less dramatically. The net result was that almost overnight, Australian wine became one of the most attractive of all investment commodities — a far cry from the situation in the 1970s and 1980s.

Late in 1997, a book was published which will remain the bible for determining the value of Australian wines for years to come, particularly if (as expected) it is periodically updated. Langton's *Australian Fine Wine Investment Guide 1998* not only provides a vintage-by-vintage, wine-by-wine list of the auction prices realised by all the best Australian wines, but incorporates 40 pages of insightful editorial into all the factors which have served to make wine the investment phenomenon of the second half of the 1990s. And it pulls no punches, as this excerpt from the introduction vividly demonstrates:

Until recently Penfolds Grange Hermitage, an auction market staple, has been the most reliable performer in Australia. The 1990 vintage of this wine has also seen a bizarre interest from investors with prices almost quadrupling in just two and a half years. Media and even economic analysts such as Access Economics in Canberra fuel the fire by not reporting the real story. The need for 'gee whiz cor blimey' anecdotes titillate the public. Far too much attention is given to far too few wines. The 1971 Grange is used as a benchmark for investment wine. It continues to outperform race horses and taxi plates, Australian shares and bonds and other investments. The fact that there are so few bottles out there in the market and that it is one particular vintage is not reported. The public are misled appallingly by the media, not to deceive them purposely, rather to show them that the world is an absurd place. There is no real understanding of what really drives the market and why some wines appreciate in value and others don't. The market is small but appears to be growing. Like all new and exciting markets it attracts a broad church. The hyperbole, over-confidence and outright greed are a new and unattractive feature of the secondary wine market. The most disturbing aspect is that few people really have an understanding of what is going on. The great human capacity for hope can delude and deceive the small investor. We receive calls every day that meet moderate to bitter levels of disappointment. Those who invested in the collectors ports during the late 1970s are still sitting on wines of very little value.

Today the need to add value to product has meant that wine producers are providing modern mythologies and stories to make their wine more desirable. Some will succeed in capturing the imagination of the wine consumer. Many, however, will not. As with the collectors ports of the '70s and '80s some investors will be disappointed. Potential, however spectacular it might appear today, may not be realised in the future. The wine-lover's world is littered with dreamers and enthusiasts.

asia: the great unknown

Internationally, fine wine prices have now risen continuously — and increasingly steeply — for 25 years. Never before has this happened, and sooner or later the run must surely come to an end. The unknown factor, however, is the shift in world economic power away from Europe and North America to Asia. The Asian economic malaise of 1997 may well intensify, and may even trigger the next world recession earlier than even the economic Jeremiahs had predicted, but in the medium term (by 2020), the GDP of Asia will exceed that of the whole of the world.

The vast population and the high disposable income of Asian wine buyers will create a wine market far greater than that which currently exists in the rest of the world. This Asian market is likewise presently only in embryonic form; it will take 10 or possibly 20 years to build distribution infrastructure and for the dissemination of basic wine information to occur. But the Internet, travel, and the increasingly cross-cultural mix of all aspects of lifestyle will do the rest. It is thus most certain that we are witnessing a fundamental shift in the value placed on fine wine and the markets in which it will be sold.

The implications for the Australian wine industry are profound. Australia has already made it clear that it sees itself as part of Asia; indeed the balance of trade already makes any discussion on the subject redundant. Australia is thus uniquely positioned to take advantage of emerging Asian market, and it is inevitable that in the early part of the next millennium it is to Asia that most Australian wine will head.

If prices for our better wines are to remain within the reach of average Australians, production will need to continue to increase at double digit percentage rates well into the next century. If it does not, Asian demand for fine Australian wine will likely cause it to join the ranks of abalone, lobster, mullet roe and tuna and become an exotic luxury for the rich.

In the meantime, the alarm bells are ringing, and it would be hard to argue with those who, in late 1997 or early 1998, took the view that the market was severely overpriced.

if you decide to sell

Let us then assume that, like the New York millionaire, you start selling as the liftboy starts buying, and you wish to turn one form of liquid asset into another. In Australia, the legal avenues to do so are very limited. Unless you are dead, bankrupt or a licensed wine merchant, it is illegal to seek to sell wine to the public. Indeed, it is illegal even to sell it to a licensed wine merchant, although this is a law more frequently ignored than observed. The principal avenues for private sale in both England and Australia are the wine auctions, which I have described in Chapter 3 when discussing their role in buying wine for the cellar.

In Australia, at least, auctions are in bad times the only legal avenue for sale if you decide you have made a mistake, or if the Commissioner of Taxation, a divorced spouse or the sudden demise of the gold index catches you unprepared. Auctioneers will both provide an estimate of the likely realisation price per bottle, and accept reasonable reserve prices. At the time of writing, times are, of course, good, and it is far more likely you will be having recourse to the auction system to realise the extraordinary profits available to those who purchased any of the blue chip wines over the past decade.

On the other side of the coin, the cooking pot, the barbecue, the local Boy Scout raffle and disliked relatives of one's husband or wife are other classic avenues for disposing of unwanted bottles. Just remember, however, that if you give a despised bottle away, it may be served in triumph to you next time you come to dinner.

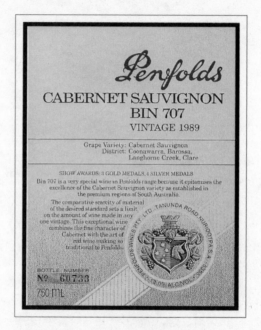

Penfolds Bin 707 Cabernet Sauvignon
Blessed with the Penfolds stamp and made with
the same uncompromising commitment to
quality as is Grange. This is a cellaring certainty
for 20-plus years.

the rewards of
the cellar

am far from sure that I should include this chapter. However hard I try, I am afraid that it will all appear sickeningly self-indulgent. On the other hand, the wine dinners and the wine tastings which I briefly recount did all take place (among a myriad of others), and are a simple reflection of the fact that I and a number of like-minded friends have always preferred to share great bottles with as many people as possible.

The greatest tastings, indeed, have been drawn not from a single cellar, but from the cellars of a dozen or so of us. In this way it is possible to bring together a wine selection which would be out of the reach of all but a handful of collectors in the United States, Belgium, Germany and England. These tasting dinners were the brainchild of Len Evans, and we (the attendees) became known as The Single Bottle Club.

But before I venture into the extraordinary series of Single Bottle Club dinners, I first look at simpler wine dinners at home. Long ago, I came to the conclusion that there should always be a menu listing both the food and the wine. I believe a home dinner party should be just that, and not a blind tasting exercise that inevitably concentrates the conversation into a single channel — which is almost certainly of little interest to the majority of guests. No matter how much thought has gone into the wine selection, and no matter how proud you are of that selection, the wine is simply there to be enjoyed. If it is to be deified, the appropriate forum is a formal wine tasting with scoresheets, water, cheese and biscuits, and a strict silence until the tasting is over, when the merits (or otherwise) of the wines in question can be discussed.

Nor do I accept for one moment the view put forward by some that great wine should be served only against simple food, so that it (the wine) can be appreciated in all its glory. That is just another form of the water-biscuit-cheese tasting exercise and, once again, has no validity in the confines of the dining room. Great wine deserves great food, or at least as great as you can make it.

On the other hand, I always try to introduce a theme in the selection of the wines. This may be pairings of a single vintage from different countries; vertical tastings of the same wine (in other words, a run of vintages of that wine); a varietal scheme (say, featuring chardonnay and cabernet); or a combination of several of those themes.

The May 1976 dinner, obviously enough, focused on the 1961 vintage, but contrasted the wines of France and Australia. The January '84 dinner for the late Gerard Jaboulet (he died prematurely in 1997) reflects the fact that Monsieur Jaboulet was the head of the distinguished winemaker Paul Jaboulet & Co. from the Rhône Valley where syrah reigns supreme. The Seppelt Great Western Sparkling Burgundies were all made from shiraz as, of course, is Penfolds Grange. The idea was then to contrast the other classic Australian grape variety, semillon, before finishing with our indigenous specials. The other dinners were simply excuses to put together (and drink) some of the finest wines from my cellar.

Then there are the large-scale wine tastings, usually held in a tasting room, a restaurant or a winery. They may or may not be accompanied by food; in this context I do believe that food, company and conversation all have to take the back seat. The largest in my experience, and in many ways the most memorable, was the tasting of 51 vintages of Chateau d'Yquem held in Brisbane on 17 March 1985. The wines spanned the years 1981 to 1899 and included all of the great years. It was attended by the chief executive of d'Yquem, Comte Alexandre de Lur Saluces, and his wife the Comtesse, who brought with them the unexpected addition of the 1899 vintage. It was an all-day affair: the morning session covered the years 1981 to 1946, the afternoon session 1944 to 1908. We broke for lunch at which (by comparison) *vin ordinaire* was served. Four of the greatest vintages — '55, '45, '21 and 1900 — were served with the dessert at the conclusion of the formal dinner that evening, with the unscheduled addition of the Lur Saluces' gift of the 1899.

Another highly memorable tasting was hosted by Madame Lalou Bize-Leroy, co-owner of the Domaine de la Romanée-Conti. It was a tasting of 36 red burgundies of the 1964 vintage, all bottled under the Leroy label. Incongruously, it was held not in Burgundy but at Chappellet Vineyard in the Napa Valley, California on Friday, 4 May 1984. The food on this occasion was very much in evidence, having been devised and cooked by the famous American chef, Jeremiah Tower. It was also a tasting very much in the French tradition: there were no spitting buckets provided. Nor were any provided at the following year's Leroy tasting, this time at the home of Madame Bize-Leroy in Auvenay, where we were treated to a similar number of burgundies, but this time with the theme being a twin vertical tasting of Mazis-Chambertin and Charmes-Chambertin going back to the 1930s.

After such leviathan exercises, only a tasting of every vintage of Latour from 1934 to 1978 (split into two nights) comes close in terms of size. But size is not everything; the dinner tasting of over 20 vintages of Pétrus (again with all the great classic years represented including the fabulous run of '45, '47, '48, '49 and '53) will never fade from my memory. And of course even if, contrary to expectations, that memory were to fade, there are always the tasting notes.

Creating the tasting notes serves two functions: they not only act as a permanent record and reminder, but they also sharpen the analytical process, forcing the taster to concentrate more on the wine, to analyse all of its component parts. It will be said by some that this is akin to pinning a butterfly on a display board, that it is an unnatural process. But so, in a sense, is the formal wine tasting: unless its purpose be educative, it serves no function at all.

So it is that I have notes for dozens of tastings. A few at random are the 19 and 20 November 1994 Anders Josephson tasting of every vintage of Grange between 1951 and 1990; on 2 May and on 23 May 1971 respectively another Latour dinner (10 vintages each night) covering the years 1959 to 1926; on 3 June 1970 a twin vertical dinner tasting of Chateau Margaux and Chateau Haut-Brion covering the years 1965 to 1920; and on 31 August 1971 a Lafite tasting offering the years '66, '62, '61, '53, '47, '45, '37, '34 and '28.

Finally, there are the magnificent Yalumba Museum tastings held in conjunction with the Barossa Vintage Festival. This invitation–only tasting invariably offers a catholic cross-section of extremely rare aged Australian wine and rarities from overseas.

The greatest tasting dinners I have been involved in have, without question, been those organised by The Single Bottle Club. As the name suggests, each person attending produces a bottle; as the years have gone by, the number of wines at the dinner (and also, it must be said, the number of people attending) has increased somewhat, and it is not at all uncommon for two or three bottles to be produced by various of the guests.

The first of the dinners was held on 4 February 1977, and I wonder whether the classic simplicity of that dinner will ever be surpassed. There have been dinners with more wine, even dinners with older wine (that of 9 September 1980, again held at Len Evans', climaxed with 1646 Tokay), but I somehow doubt that there has ever been or ever will be a better dinner.

old wines, kid gloves

The question then arises how one handles and serves wines of such extreme age. Under ideal circumstances, they should be moved with as little disturbance as possible to the room where they will ultimately be decanted, and served, a week — and preferably two — before service. They should be left standing upright and should not even be touched during the ensuing weeks.

If the room is too warm, or prying eyes and fiddling fingers too common, some other interim storage will have to be devised. If for any reason you have to take an old wine to a dinner for immediate service, there is a major problem. The late Ronald Avery neatly solved this by opening the bottle in his cellar, decanting it into another bottle, and eliminating the ullage (the original bottle will undoubtedly have murky sediment which has to be discarded) by filling the bottle in which the decanted wine is placed with enough small glass marbles to eliminate the air space which would otherwise exist.

Then there is the question of how long wines should be opened before they are served. There are two schools of thought. One holds that you can wait for an old wine, but an old wine cannot wait for you. In other words, it is difficult to predict just how a very old wine will appear when first poured: there may be the musty odours of extreme bottle age which will disappear with time as the fruit comes up, or there may be an immediate ethereal fragrance. Even less predictable is the durability of the aroma: some old wines flower for but a few minutes, others seem to unfold in the glass for hours and hours.

The alternative school of thought holds fairly robustly to the view that most old wines benefit from some period of aeration. Whether this be 30 minutes, one hour or (idiosyncratically, but nonetheless practised by a few in Bordeaux) 24 hours is a matter partly of personal judgement, and hopefully partly dependent on prior knowledge of the wine in question.

In fact, I think it is possible to have the best of both worlds: if it is an old wine (30 years or more) open it 30 minutes before service. Smell the bottle, having scrupulously cleaned the neck to remove any slime or dirt which might give a misleading impression. If the wine smells sweet and fragrant, partially reinsert the cork, or if it is old and broken, a fresh clean cork. If on the other hand there does appear to be a fair degree of bottle stink (as the expression goes) or the wine appears closed, decant it forthwith. The aeration induced by decanting accelerates the development process.

the technique of decanting

Whatever the outcome, it is essential that old wines be decanted. Leaving the bottle in one of those little wicker or wire baskets is an abomination: it simply ensures that the sediment, which will extend along the side of the bottle, is stirred up and spread through the wine by the time the first glass has been poured. Sediment of this kind has a very unsettling effect, spreading a muddy taste and clouding the otherwise crystal clarity of an old wine.

The process of decanting is largely a matter of commonsense. If the bottle has been left standing upright (and undisturbed) for a week or more, the sediment will have collected at the base, making the task so much easier. If the bottle has just come from the cellar, it may still be at least partially spread along the bottom side of the bottle underneath the label (assuming the label has been uppermost in the cellar).

Because of this distribution, there are those who bring the bottle from the cellar to the table in the basket I so despise. As I say, I think this is ill-conceived: the 'sloshing' effect achieved when a bottle is moved while on its side is far greater than the movement of the contents in a bottle carried in an upright position. Further sloshing occurs when the cork is removed from the bottle held on its side, unless the operator is both lucky and extremely skilful.

Whether the bottle to be decanted starts in a vertical or near-horizontal position, the rules are the same. The labels should be uppermost as the decanting procedure takes place; once the pouring starts, it should proceed gently and slowly, and should not under any circumstances be interrupted, and never should the bottle be brought upright before it is empty.

Traditionalists will place a candle on the decanting table, modernists a torch. The neck of the bottle being decanted should be positioned so that, once the bottle is nearing emptiness and has come to a semi-horizontal position, the light will be directly underneath the shallow stream of wine passing along the parallel sides of the neck. Dirt, fixed sediment and the distance between the walls of the glass in the body of the bottle will obscure the contents in that portion of the bottle, particularly if it is an old one.

A light, slightly milky sediment will usually appear first. Here experience comes into play: a knowledge of the wine and a quick glance at the bottom of the bottle (not easy because one's hand will largely obscure it and the light will be no great help) will determine whether the decanting process should continue for a second or two or be discontinued forthwith. If in doubt, discontinue it.

sediment: sometimes worth saving

If that course be taken, and if there still seems to be a significant amount of precious wine in the bottle, hold the bottle in the same semi-vertical position and continue pouring the remainder (until the sediment is obviously too thick) into a separate vessel, be it a glass, or jug — it should not have too large a surface area on its bottom. This will resettle, and an extra glass or so (usually not up to the standard of the wine in the decanter, mind you) may be saved. Candlelight at the dinner table and the goodwill generated by a great dinner party may even cause that glass to taste like ambrosia.

Handling a bottle in this fashion is not difficult for the expert. A magnum is much less easy: the hand holding the magnum becomes tired, and you need either a magnum decanter or two decanters side by side and a sure eye and steady hand as you move from decanter one to decanter two.

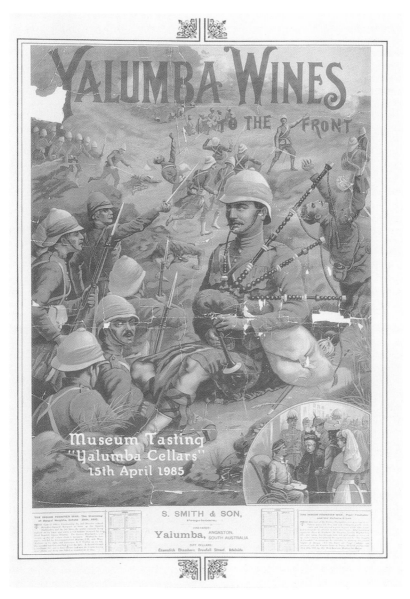

This brochure accompanied a memorable tasting I attended at the Yalumba Museum, 15 April 1985.

Some of the wines that were part of the special tasting at the Yalumba Museum on 27 April 1981 — from left: 1825 Tokay Essence; 1880 Malmsey Madeira; Old Four Crown Port; 1942 Mount Pleasant TY Hermitage; and 1935 Yalumba Carte D'or Riesling. *Courtesy Yalumba Wines*

A stock of old Carte D'or Rieslings now held in Yalumba's wine museum.
Courtesy Yalumba Wines

One of the historic underground drives at Seppelt's Great Western winery.
Courtesy Seppelt Wines

The finest sherry outside of Spain is made in Australia's Barossa Valley.
Milton Wordley/Wildlight

Cellarack's systems come in all shapes and sizes.
Courtesy Cellarack

The cask room, with traditional earthen floor, at Tyrrell's winery, Hunter Valley. Murray and Bruce Tyrrell are standing in the background. *Courtesy Tymson Communications*

Old bottles in Thomas Hardy's famous 'black hole' museum.

Riddling racks for sparkling wine production, old but effective.
Milton Wordley/Wildlight

O, for a draught of vintage! that hath been
Cool'd a long age in the deep-delved earth.
John Keats, *Ode to a Nightingale*

A decanting funnel, with a curved spout which directs the wine against the side of the decanter, is a useful adjunct whether one is dealing with a bottle or a magnum. Never, however, rely on the sieve in the top to strain sediment: it is useful to catch the odd piece of cork which may be floating in the wine, but nothing else. Nor is a muslin cloth or a coffee filter paper recommended as a substitute for careful decanting: experience shows they either do not work at all, or that the cure is worse than the illness.

large bottles and other oddities

Moving from a magnum to a double magnum or larger container (holding four, six, eight or even 12 bottles) brings special problems which I once saw Jacques Seysses, owner of Domaine Dujac in Burgundy, deal with most expertly. He placed a small siphon tube into the bottom of the imperial and siphoned the lees off the bottom, leaving the rest of the wine undisturbed. Simplicity itself, as is all lateral thinking.

It also strictly accorded with the classical Burgundian view which frowns on decanting under any circumstances. I have recounted attending several magnificent formal tastings staged by Madame Lalou Bize-Leroy. She refused to decant her wines, which were poured at the table after we were seated by waiters in the usual way. If you were lucky and received one of the first few glasses from the bottle, all was well. If you received the last glass, you were in deep trouble with the older wines in the tasting. The Burgundians believe the aroma of their wine is so precious and so delicate it must not be imperilled by decanting.

If you were a Bordelaise confronted by a very large bottle of old wine, and wished to decant it, the siphon tube would still be used, but you would 'rack' the wine exactly as winemakers rack young wines from barrel to barrel. You would draw the clear wine off the top, progressively lowering the siphon until only the sediment remained in the bottom.

Old wine is a wonderful thing. Generations will have been involved in its production, and history will have been made and written as it matured. Thus it was a profoundly emotional experience to share in the bottle of 1646 Tokay, and to think that while it was being made Cromwell's Roundheads were stalking the English countryside.

Such are the rewards of the cellar.

australian wines
vintage chart

1 – Worst Vintage

10 – Best Vintage

	'87	'88	'89	'90	'91	'92	'93	'94	'95	'96	'97
new south wales											
Riverina/Griffith											
red	6	6	5	8	7	9	7	6	8	9	8
white	6	6	5	8	7	8	8	7	8	8	8
Orange											
red	5	6	5	8	6	8	6	8	7	9	8
white	7	6	5	7	7	9	7	7	8	8	9
Mudgee											
red	5	6	7	8	7	6	5	8	6	8	8
white	7	7	9	8	8	6	7	8	7	8	7
Lower Hunter Valley											
red	9	4	5	4	10	4	5	7	5	6	7
white	8	4	5	6	8	8	5	6	7	8	4
Upper Hunter Valley											
red	8	7	8	5	9	5	6	7	8	9	7
white	6	7	7	6	9	6	7	7	8	9	7
Hastings River											
red	8	8	7	4	7	6	8	6	7	5	5
white	6	6	8	5	6	6	8	7	8	6	8

australian wines vintage chart *continued*

	'87	'88	'89	'90	'91	'92	'93	'94	'95	'96	'97
victoria											
Bendigo											
red	7	9	6	10	8	8	6	8	7	9	10
white	7	8	7	9	6	8	5	7	6	8	9
Goulburn Valley											
red	8	7	5	8	9	8	6	7	8	7	9
white	7	8	6	7	6	9	6	8	7	8	6
Gippsland											
red	7	9	6	8	9	8	6	9	8	7	9
white	8	9	6	6	9	8	7	8	8	6	8
Glenrowan and Rutherglen											
red	6	8	4	7	7	8	5	7	5	8	5
white	6	8	6	7	7	8	6	7	6	5	5
King Valley											
red	6	8	4	7	7	8	5	7	5	6	5
white	6	8	6	7	7	8	6	7	6	5	5
Geelong											
red	6	8	6	9	7	8	6	8	9	8	8
white	8	8	7	7	8	8	8	9	9	8	8
Macedon											
red	6	8	6	9	9	7	8	8	8	7	8
white	7	8	5	9	9	7	8	8	8	6	7
Mornington Peninsula											
red	7	9	6	8	8	7	10	8	7	5	10
white	7	8	6	7	8	7	9	9	8	7	8
Yarra Valley											
red	7	10	5	8	10	10	7	9	7	8	9
white	6	10	4	8	8	10	8	9	5	7	8
Far South-West Victoria											
red	6	8	7	8	8	8	9	8	7	8	8
white	8	9	9	8	8	9	7	9	8	9	8
Grampians											
red	5	8	7	7	9	8	9	9	10	9	10
white	7	7	6	8	7	8	7	7	9	7	9
Pyrenees											
red	7	10	6	10	10	8	8	8	8	10	7
white	7	9	6	7	9	8	8	7	8	10	7

australian wines vintage chart *continued*

	'87	'88	'89	'90	'91	'92	'93	'94	'95	'96	'97
south australia											
Adelaide											
red	7	8	5	8	10	9	7	8	9	8	9
white	8	8	6	9	9	8	8	8	8	9	9
Barossa Valley											
red	6	7	7	9	8	7	8	8	7	9	8
white	7	8	7	9	8	7	7	8	8	9	7
Eden Valley											
red	6	7	7	10	8	8	8	9	7	9	7
white	9	6	6	9	6	7	7	7	8	8	9
McLaren Vale											
red	7	8	7	10	9	9	8	9	8	9	7
white	8	8	6	10	9	9	8	9	8	9	7
Coonawarra											
red	6	7	6	10	9	6	8	9	6	9	7
white	6	8	6	7	7	6	8	9	7	9	6
Padthaway											
red	5	8	5	7	7	5	6	9	6	8	6
white	7	5	7	8	9	7	8	10	8	9	8
Adelaide Hills											
red	5	9	4	9	9	7	6	8	8	9	7
white	6	7	4	7	6	9	6	7	8	9	7
Clare Valley											
red	8	8	6	10	8	8	7	8	7	7	8
white	9	7	5	10	7	7	8	9	8	7	10
western australia											
Swan District											
red	5	5	6	6	8	6	7	6	6	6	7
white	9	6	7	7	10	6	10	7	7	6	5
Great Southern											
red	6	8	8	10	9	8	7	10	9	8	7
white	7	8	7	9	7	8	7	9	8	8	9
Margaret River											
red	8	8	6	7	10	8	7	9	9	9	8
white	8	7	6	8	8	8	9	8	9	8	6

australian wines vintage chart *continued*

	'87	'88	'89	'90	'91	'92	'93	'94	'95	'96	'97
tasmania											
Northern Tasmania											
red	5	7	6	7	8	8	5	8	9	7	8
white	7	7	8	8	9	9	8	9	9	7	9
Southern Tasmania											
red	6	8	6	9	7	8	9	9	8	5	8
white	6	8	7	8	7	8	9	8	9	6	8
queensland											
red	8	8	10	9	9	8	10	10	9	9	
white	8	7	9	8	8	8	9	9	9	10	
canberra											
red	6	9	6	8	9	7	8	8	9	8	8
white	7	9	5	8	8	7	7	6	8	8	8

european wines vintage chart

1 – Worst Vintage

10 – Best Vintage

(NV = *non vintage, vintage not declared*)

	'86	'87	'88	'89	'90	'91	'92	'93	'94	'95	'96
france											
Bordeaux											
white	10	4	10	9	10	5	5	5	6	8	8
red	9	6	8	9	10	4	5	7	7	9	9
Burgundy											
white	6	7	8	9	9	6	10	7	8	10	9
red	5	7	8	9	10	6	6	8	7	9	10
Rhône Valley											
red	7	7	9	10	10	9	5	4	7	9	7
Alsace											
white	7	7	8	10	10	5	8	8	10	9	8
Loire											
white	8	6	8	10	10	5	7	8	8	8	10
Champagne											
white	9	NV	9	9	10	NV	NV	8	NV	9	10
germany											
Rhine Mosel											
white	6	7	8	9	10	7	9	8	9	8	10

European Wines Vintage Chart *continued*

	'86	'87	'88	'89	'90	'91	'92	'93	'94	'95	'96
portugal											
vintage port	NV	NV	NV	NV	NV	9	10	NV	10	NV	—
Italy											
Piedmont											
red	5	7	9	10	10	5	8	6	9	10	—
Tuscany											
red	5	9	5	10	8	5	8	8	9	6	—

auctioneers

united kingdom

Christie's

The world's leading wine auctioneers. Catalogues available by annual subscription or can be purchased individually in England. Many of the catalogues are works of art and collector's items in themselves.

Subscription enquiries to Christie's Publications
21–25 South Lambeth Road, London, SW8 ISX. **fax** 44 171 389 2869

Sotheby's

Next in importance to Christie's, and in recent years competing vigorously for business. Auctions of similar frequency to Christie's (weekly or fortnightly in 'the season') and wines of similar variety and rarity.

Subscription enquiries to Sotheby's
34–35 New Bond Street, London, W1. **fax** 44 171 408 5989

australia

Langton's Fine Wine Auctions
(in association with Christie's)

Australia's leading wine auctioneers, holding regular sales in both Sydney and Melbourne. Andrew Caillard MW presides over Sydney, Stuart Langton over Melbourne.

7 Claremont Street, South Yarra, Vic 3141
phone (03) 9824 0088 **fax** (03) 9824 0288.
52 Pitt Street, Redfern, NSW 2016
phone (02) 9310 4231 **fax** (02) 9310 4236

Lawson's

Sydney's oldest auction house, offering a wide selection of Australian,
French and New Zealand wine.
212 Cumberland Street, Sydney, NSW 2000
phone (02) 9241 3411 **fax** (02) 9251 5869

National Auction Group

Canberra wine auctioneers. Previously relied on the absence of licence
fees in the ACT, an advantage that ceased in 1997.
41A Whyalla Street, Fyshwick, ACT 2609
phone (02) 6280 4400 **fax** (02) 6280 5111

Oddbins Wine Auctions

Oddbins is run by well-known Adelaide auctioneer Colin Gaetjens, who
has for years conducted the fine wine auction forming part of the Barossa
Vintage Festival.
Enquiries to Colin Gaetjens & Co.
2 Grenfell Street, Kent Town, SA 5067
phone (08) 8362 4700 **fax** (08) 8362 3355

Richardson's Wine Auctions

Regularly holds auctions in Adelaide, always offering significant quantities
of Penfolds Grange and other premium wines.
15 Kingston Avenue, Richmond, SA 5033
phone (08) 8351 7373 **fax** (08) 8351 7374

Sterling Wine Auctioneers

929 Hay Street, Perth, WA 6000
phone (08) 9481 7811 **fax** (08) 9481 5229

societies

Cellarmasters

Cellarmasters is the largest of all the direct mail wine–selling operations in Australia, with a membership of over 260 000. It was acquired by Mildara Blass in 1997. The annual membership fee is $25. Cellarmasters accepts all major credit cards. A carefully selected and very keenly priced portfolio of wines, sometimes under standard commercial labels, more often under producer labels which are exclusive to Cellarmasters. Also makes limited offers of premium wines to its top customers. A sophisticated computer program lies at the heart of this extremely successful business.

Membership enquiries (and orders) to:
freecall 1800 505 250, **freefax** 1800 500 320

David Jones Wine Club

Membership of this club is largely based upon David Jones account holders, but having an account is not a prerequisite — membership of the club is open to all. Current membership is around 4500, and there are no joining fees or annual subscriptions. The only requirement is that at least one case of wine per year be purchased. The author selects all of the wines for the Wine Club, and provides detailed tasting notes of 24 wines selected each month in the bi-monthly newsletter.

Membership enquiries to David Jones Wine Club
GPO Box 503, Sydney, NSW 2000
phone (02) 9266 5500

The Wine Society

The Wine Society is Australia's largest non-profit wine society, and the oldest of the direct mail operations, having been established in 1946. The once-only membership fee is $50, being payment for 25 shares in the co-operative society at $2 per share. The bi-monthly mailing list offers a good selection of wines both under commercial labels and under The Wine Society's own label. The prices offer a discount on recommended retail prices, and the society has been much revived in recent years by more energetic management and better wine selection than in the past.
Membership applications to The Wine Society,
177 Cathedral Street, Woolloomooloo, NSW 2011
phone (02) 9356 4000

magazines

australia

Australian Gourmet Traveller Wine

First published October 1997, with the promise of becoming Australia's most important wine magazine. Initially to be published quarterly, but with plans to go bi-monthly. Cover price $6.95, NZ$8.95. Annual subscription rates $22 domestic, $44 overseas.
Subscriptions to *Australian Gourmet Traveller Wine*
GPO Box 5252, Sydney, NSW 1028
fax (02) 9267 4363

Divine

Eclectic but informative (and advertising free) wine and food magazine published quarterly by publishing editor Andrew Wood and contributing editor Max Allen. Subscription rates $34, $65 overseas airmail.
Subscriptions to *Divine*
3 Charles Street, St Kilda, Vic 3182,
fax (03) 9534 1998
Also available through selected fine wine and food retailers in Victoria, New South Wales and South Australia.

Jeremy Oliver OnWine

Issued bi-monthly and contains tasting notes of new releases, detailed illustrated feature articles, wine industry facts, industry news, a wine diary, interviews with opinion leaders and notes on wines to purchase. Also published on the Internet (http//onwine.com.au).

Annual subscription rate $59.

Details from Jeremy Oliver

565 Burwood Road, Hawthorn, Vic 3122

phone (03) 9819 4400 **fax** (03) 9819 5322

Winestate

Australia's longest established specialist wine magazine published bi-monthly. Each issue contains feature articles, special regional tastings, and new-release tastings. Cover price $6.95; widely distributed through newsagents. Annual subscription rates $39, $58 overseas.

Subscriptions to *Winestate* Publications

81 King William Road, Unley, SA 5061

fax (08) 8357 9212

Winewise

Published bi-monthly. Single colour, usually 24 pages. No advertising. An acerbic tasting magazine with no feature articles. Tastings cover selected current releases, vertical tastings of selected vineyards and style tastings. Subscription only: Australia $45, $60 overseas airmail.

Subscriptions to *Winewise*

PO Box 391, Belconnen, ACT 2616

fax (02) 6255 1745

Others

There are a number of specialist magazines, with a greater or lesser degree of technical or trade orientation. These include:

Australian and New Zealand Wine Industry Journal.

Published quarterly. High quality presentation. 72 pages. Available by subscription only at $69 annually including postage; overseas $90 (economy airmail).

Subscription enquiries to PO Box 1140, Marlestone, SA 5033

Australian Grape Grower & Winemaker

The industry's basic journal. A little pedestrian in its content, but excellent annual technical issue. Printed in colour, usually 62 pages.

Industry news and advertising. Published monthly. Subscription rates $55 Australia and New Zealand.

Subscription enquiries to Ryan Publications

95 Currie Street, Adelaide, SA 5000

united kingdom

Decanter

Published monthly. Large format full-colour magazine usually around 120 pages. Regarded as one of the foremost general wine magazines in the world. Extensive coverage of wines from all countries. Tastings and tasting notes less formalised than Australian or American magazines. Cover price £2.95. Annual subscriptions £92 surface mail, £144 airmail.

Subscription enquiries to *Decanter* Subscriptions

Bradley Pavilions, Pear Tree Road, Bradley Stoke North, Bristol BS12 OBQ

Wine

Published monthly. Large format, slightly above A4, around 82 pages, with abundant colour. Similar to *Decanter*, but with rather more emphasis on tastings. A good alternative to *Decanter* for the general consumer. Each year's October mammoth issue (226 pages) gives results of the International Wine Challenge, held in London in May under the auspices of the magazine and which is the largest (6700 entries) wine competition in the world. Cover price £2.95.

Annual Australia and New Zealand subscription £60 airmail.

Enquiries to *Wine* Subscriptions

PO Box 219, Woking, GU21 1ZW

united states

The Wine Advocate

Published monthly. Produced by the redoubtable and indefatigable Robert M Parker, assisted since late 1996 by Pierre Antoine Rovani. Single-colour, 48-page format with tasting notes; no advertisements and no feature articles. Covers all the wines of the world in hyperbolic prose and flamboyant use of the 100-point scale.

Subscription rates $US85 for foreign airmail. Credit cards accepted.

Subscriptions to *The Wine Advocate*

PO Box 311, Monkton MD 21111

Wine Spectator

Probably the most influential magazine in the world, published twice each month in large A5 format, with extensive colour photography. 184 full colour pages, with detailed tasting notes and points on a 100-point scale similar to that used by *The Wine Advocate*. *Wine Spectator* is compulsive (and compulsory) reading, covering an extraordinarily wide range of topics in each issue. Subscription rates US$125 second class airmail.

Subscription enquiries to *Wine Spectator*

PO Box 50463, Boulder Co 80323–0463

Wines & Vines

Published monthly. Principal trade magazine in the United States. Usually around 90 pages. Some colour but principally black and white. Orientated much more to industry and trade than consumer.

Subscription rates US$50 surface mail, US$85 airmail.

Subscriptions to by Hiaring Company

1800 Lincoln Avenue, San Rafael California 94901–1298

new zealand

Cuisine

Published bi-monthly. Full-colour, glossy presentation, usually 144 pages. Covers both food and wine, both in considerable depth. Certainly the best general publication wine magazine in New Zealand. Cover price NZ$7.95.

Annual subscription rates NZ$70 surface mail.

Enquiries to *Cuisine*

PO Box 37–349, Parnell, Auckland

books

Bradley, Robin *Australian and New Zealand Wine Vintages,* Robin Bradley, Melbourne, 1998 (15th edition).
The original vintage guide to Australasian wines with an extremely detailed rating on a wine-by-wine, vintage-by-vintage basis of the majority of the fine wines of Australasia. The ratings are entirely numeric, with no text, but the pocket-size format proves very popular.

Broadbent, Michael *The Great Vintage Wine Book II,* Mitchell Beazley, London, 1991.
After a gap of 11 years, the second edition of *The Great Vintage Wine Book* appeared in 1991. It is the most comprehensive book of its kind in the world, with tasting notes on all of the great classic wines most people are likely to encounter, and a great number of wines (from earlier centuries) which only a handful of people in the world will get the chance to taste. Gives a vintage-by-vintage and wine-by-wine description of all of the major wine-producing regions (including a few Australian entries), but with a heavy concentration on the classics of France. Absolutely essential for those seriously interested in assembling a cellar of old classic wines.

Caillard, Andrew & Langton, Stewart *Langton's Australian Fine Wine Investment Guide 1998,* G & O Publishing, Sydney.
After a gap of seven years, a comprehensive and up-to-date listing of the auction prices of all the major Australian wines arranged vintage by vintage. Also highly entertaining and interesting editorial comment. Quite indispensable. $24.95 from G & O Publishing Partners, PO Box 1638, Bondi Junction, NSW 2022. **phone** (02) 9387 3266

Clarke, Oz (ed) *Oz Clarke's Wine Guide,* Websters/Mitchell Beazley, London.
An annual guide to price and availability, together with vintage information, tasting notes and statistical overview. An immense amount of information is included which is of interest even in Australia although the major use is clearly in the UK market.

Cooper, Michael *Buyer's Guide to New Zealand Wine 1988,* Hodder Moa Beckett, Auckland.
A wine-by-wine tasting note and rating of 1250 of New Zealand's best wines.

Halliday, James *A History of the Australian Wine Industry 1949–1994,* Winetitles, Adelaide, 1994.
Concise history of the industry, with voluminous statistics, graphs and charts.

Halliday, James *Classic Wines of Australia,* HarperCollins*Publishers*, Sydney, 1998 (2nd edition).
Second edition, with vertical tasting notes of 90 of Australia's greatest wines including Grange 1951–1992, McWilliam's O'Shea reds 1937–1954, Woodley Coonawarra 1930–1954, Seppelt Para Ports 1878–1994, Henschke Hill of Grace 1959–1993.

Halliday, James *James Halliday's Australia and New Zealand Wine Companion, 1998 Edition,* Angus & Robertson, Sydney.
Published annually, this is an A–Z listing to every winery in Australia and New Zealand with tasting notes and details of 1000 individual wines.

Halliday, James *Wine Atlas of Australia and New Zealand,* HarperCollins*Publishers*, Sydney, 1998 (2nd edition).
Large format, full-colour throughout. The entirely rewritten second edition will be the most comprehensive and up-to-date reference work on Australian and New Zealand wines/regions when published in late 1998.

Halliday, James *Wine Atlas of California,* Angus & Robertson, Sydney, 1993.
Large-format, full-colour throughout. Multi-award-winning book — awards include *Wine Spectator* Book of the Year, the James Beard Award and the Julia Child IACP award.

Halliday, James & Johnson, Hugh *The Art and Science of Wine,* Mitchell Beazley, London, 1992.
Multi-award-winning full-colour, large format book describing the wine styles of the world, tracing them from vineyard to winery to bottle to cellar.

Hook, Huon & Shield, Mark *The Good Australian Wine Guide,* Penguin Australia, 1997.
A–Z tasting notes and rating of 1000 Australian wines, soft cover.

Johnson, Hugh *Pocket Wine Book '97,* Mitchell Beazley, London.
The best-selling wine book in the world, year in, year out. World coverage.

Johnson, Hugh *World Atlas of Wine Fourth Edition,* Mitchell Beazley, London, 1994.
Simply the ultimate introduction to the wines of the world. A classic work that will never date, but is nonetheless revised from time to time, as it was in 1994.

Joseph, Robert *Good Wine Guide 1997,* Dorling Kindersley, London.
This is a densely packed guide that contains 2500 entries on grape varieties, regions, producers and terms, along with 1500 buying recommendations.

Oliver, Jeremy *Australian Wine Annual,* OnWine Publications, Melbourne, 1998.
The 1998 edition is in a new format, finally moving away from the work of Robin Bradley. Contains numeric rating of thousands of Australian wines with clever maturity coding (indicated by use of colour). Self published. Contact 565 Burwood Road, Hawthorn, Vic 3122. Soft-cover.

Robinson, Jancis *Oxford Companion to Wine,* Oxford University Press, 1994.

If you have only one wine book in your possession, this should be it. Over 3000 entries (A–Z) in 1088 pages covering every conceivable aspect of wine.

Robinson, Jancis *Vines, Grapes and Wines,* Mitchell Beazley, London, 1986.

Strictly outside the subject of tasting notes and cellaring, but the ultimate work on grape varieties and varietal wines. Included for its sheer quality. Reprinted 1996 in handy pocket book format.

Williams, Vic *The Penguin Good New Zealand Wine Guide 1997/98,* Penguin, Auckland.

The New Zealand equivalent to the Australian book by Huon Hooke and Mark Shield. wine-by-wine description, rating and tasting notes.

cellar racking systems and self storage

Bordex Wine Racks

Outlets in the following states:
South Australia **phone** (08) 8340 1660
Victoria **phone** (03) 9882 1022
New South Wales **phone** (019) 622 935
Western Australia **phone** (08) 9298 8122
Available in modular kits or custom-made; the original, and arguably most beautiful, individual bottle storage system with wooden corner-pieces joined by flat steel inserts. Available in virtually any size or configuration.

Cellarack Wine Racks

Outlets in the following states:
South Australia, Home Storage Shop, 643 Magill Road, Magill, 5072
phone (08) 8364 0465 **fax** (08) 8364 3935
Victoria, Cnr Lower Dandenong & De Havilland Rds, Mordialloc 3195
phone (03) 9587 2282 **fax** (03) 9587 3166
New South Wales **phone** (02) 9948 6347 **fax** (02) 9948 3424
Produces coated steel racking systems in a wide variety of configurations, single bottle and triangular/diamond bulk bin shapes, all of which can be combined in self-designed modules.

Cellar Box

Tony Jackson, PO Box 1365, Collingwood, Vic 3066
phone (03) 9696 7226
A styrene 12-bottle box measuring 48 cm x 38 cm. Its significant advantage over all other systems is its insulation capacity, which is of particular interest in hot inland or tropical parts of Australia. A refrigeration component can be incorporated during heatwaves by freezing a bottle of water and storing it in one of the compartments in the box. Expensive as a racking system but not as a self-contained cellar. (As a further advantage, the box also excludes light, which means it can be stored anywhere.)

Cellarwine

phone (02) 9948 6347 **fax** (02) 9948 3424
Specialist in tailor-made installations in all types of configurations and materials from wood to coated steel; also supplies cooled wine cabinets, cellar coolers and offers full cellar construction.

The de Burgh-Day Wine Company

Building 38, Lionel Street, Essendon Airport, Vic 3041
phone (03) 5426 4188 **fax** (03) 5426 4472
Economical coated steel 12-bottle modular racks which will stack up to 10 high. Six-bottle magnum racks also available in identical external dimensions.

Prestige Cellars

149 Grove Road, Grovedale, Vic 3216
phone (03) 5244 2769 or (03) 5275 4329 **fax** (03) 5241 3622
Specialist builder and supplier of underground wine cellars providing storage from 900 to 2000 bottles. Said to be ideal under new extensions and garages.

Rack-au-Vin

PO Box 308, Brookland Park, SA 5032
phone (08) 8443 3951 **fax** (08) 8234 5004.
Economical 12- and 24-bottle coated steel modules, connected by wooden Rack-au-Vin connectors for each additional module.

The Redrak Company

Unit 6, 33B Burgess Street, Kings Beach, Qld 4551
phone (0412) 590 624
http://www.noosanetcafe.com.au/redrak
Unique fibreglass reinforced high-impact plastic racking system especially
suited for curved or round installations, but also available flat, and able to
be installed in any configuration, even triangular.

Self Storage Millers locations

Sydney 866 Bourke Street, Waterloo
phone (02) 9699 2300 **fax** (02) 9699 1700
Brisbane 98 Montpelier Road, Bowen Hills
phone (07) 3257 3224 **fax** (07) 3257 3225
Melbourne 601 Little Collins Street, Melbourne
phone (03) 9629 1122 **fax** (03) 9629 1083
Gold Coast 6 Newcastle Street, Gold Coast
phone (07) 5593 5993 **fax** (07) 5593 5915

The Wine Cellar

2/97 Jijaws St, Sumner Park, Qld 4074
phone (07) 3279 2157 **fax** (07) 3279 1621
Specialist in warm-area cellar installations, supplying cooling units and
custom-made wooden racking systems. Also supplies EuroCave
temperature and humidity-controlled wine cabinets for small cellars.

Winerax

252 Riley Street, Surry Hills, NSW 2010
phone (02) 9211 4555 **fax** (02) 9212 5609
Polythene-coated wire mesh. Standard module 61 cm x 121 cm holds 72
bottles in single-bottle storage and can be installed horizontally or
vertically.

wine on the web

There are literally thousands of websites on wine. The following list is by no means the definitive but it will give a good starting point.

James Halliday

http://www.jameshalliday.com.au
The author's site launched in early 1998, with extensive, regularly updated coverage of every aspect of the Australian and New Zealand wine industries including feature articles, tasting notes of new releases, vertical tastings, industry statistics and economies, events and tastings calendars and much more.

Jeremy Oliver OnWine

http://onwine.com.au
The Internet version of Jeremy Oliver's wine magazine issued bi-monthly, contains tasting notes of new releases, detailed illustrated articles, industry news, interviews with opinion leaders and notes on wines to purchase.

Wine of Australia

http://www.wineaustralia.com.au
Produced by the South Australian Wine & Brandy Industry Association, the site includes information on the wineries, wine regions and more.

The World-Wide Web Virtual Library: Wine

http://www.primenet.com/~frantic/html/wwwvl-wine.html
A comprehensive list of wine sites from around the world classified into topic areas such as education and research, wine societies, region-specific wine information and wineries.

Wines, Beer and Spirits of the Net

http://www.eye.nt/Food-drink/Drinks/tudor/htm
A list of alcohol-related sites on the web including wines, beers and spirits.

Wines of the World

http://www.winelink.com
A wine directory that links to the world's wineries.

Australian Journal of Grape and Wine Research

http://www.winetitles.com.au/ajgwr.html
A journal published by the Australian Society of Viticulture and Oenology.

Australian Society of Viticulture and Oenology

http://www.winetitles.com.au/asvo.html
A non-profit organisation to serve the interests of practising winemakers and viticulturists.

CSIRO Grapevine Server in Australia

http://cgswww.adl.hort.csiro.au/gwrdc.html

Grape and Wine Research and Development Corporation

http://www.winetitles.com.au/gwrdc.html
Australia's statutory body that oversees funding for research and development projects in viticulture and oenology.

Australian Society of Wine Education

http://www.winebase.com.au/aswe
Information about the society and the programs it runs.

Australian Wine Online

http://www.winetitles.com.au
This site includes information based on the Australian and New Zealand Wine Industry Journal and the Grape and Wine Research Development Corporation.

New Zealand Wines Online

http://www.nzwine.com
Information on the wines, wineries and wine regions of New Zealand.

Coldstream Hills

http://www.coldstreamhills.com.au

A virtual reality tour of Coldstream Hills, the winery established by the author and now part of Southcorp, with up-to-date tasting notes on the Coldstream Hills releases.

Australian Wines of Distinction

http://www.australianwines.com.au

An informative background to the innumerable wineries and brands which form part of the Southcorp group, Australia's largest fine wine producer, and the ninth largest in the world.

World Wine Web

http://www.winevin.com

An international encyclopedia describing the wine regions of the world.

Wine Spectator

http://www.winespectator.com

Includes over 55 000 wine reviews from around the world, as well as wine forums, polls and an archive of all *Wine Spectator* articles since 1994.

wine merchants

national

Vintage Cellars

In 1997 operated in all mainland states except Queensland (pending 1998), with 38 fine wine outlets, and hundreds more under the less fine wine oriented (but still excellent) Liquorland badge. All are part of the Coles Myer group. In each state one store carries the complete range of wines stocked by Vintage Cellars (and Liquorland), but all wines can be ordered from any store. Individual listing of the top Vintage Cellars store in each capital city appears hereunder; see also full listings in local telephone directories.

new south wales

Best Cellars

91 Crown St, East Sydney
phone (02) 9361 3733 **fax** (02) 9331 7892
David Matters presides over a thriving business based primarily on premium Australian wine, with a strong corporate client base, but also offering high quality, mainstream imported wines.

Camperdown Cellars

21 Kingston Road, Camperdown
phone (02) 9516 4466 **fax** (02) 9517 2238

A very well-known name in New South Wales retailing which, however, has had more than its fair share of ups and downs since its golden days in the 1970s under the ownership of Andrew and Hadey Simon. In July 1997 became Sydney's first Internet wine store under the direction of author/manager/wine consultant Rob Walters, who also heads Ex-Nihilo, a wine consultancy business. The cyber-store can be found at http://www.camperdown-cellars.com.au. The site offers wine for sale, wine and food matchings, and interesting graphics by Kate Sweetapple. Secure credit card transactions possible.

Figtree Cellars

231 Burns Bay Road, Lane Cove
phone (02) 9428 1899 **fax** (02) 9418 9794
High volume, keenly priced retailer that covers a very wide range of Australian wines from all regions and covering all price ranges.

Five Ways Cellars

4 Heeley St, Paddington
phone (02) 9360 4242 **fax** (02) 9360 9803
An eastern suburbs institution which deservedly enjoys an extremely loyal clientele; well chosen, well displayed wines.

Porters Liquor

35 Hill St, Roseville
phone (02) 9412 2122
156a New South Head Road Edgecliff
phone (02) 9363 4848 **fax** (02) 9363 5635
Edgecliff was once famous as Jarmans, Roseville once famous as Roseville Cellars, but both are now doing equally well under the Porters banner with top-shelf selections of Australian and imported wines at good prices. Quarterly newsletter.

The Ultimo Wine Centre

The Ultimo Wine Centre
Shop 99, 460–480 Jones St, Ultimo
phone (02) 9211 2380 **fax** (02) 9211 2382
John Osbeiston runs one of the most interesting and enterprising retail businesses in Australia. A particular specialty is direct imports from

unusual parts of the world, as well as classical regions, which are exclusive to Oddbins. Carefully selected range of super-premium and premium Australian wines. Has been in the business for a long time, and simply keeps on getting better.

The Wine Gallery

Shop 1, 211–219 Bulwara Road, Pyrmont (Cnr Upper Fig Street)
phone (02) 9552 2100 **fax** (02) 9552 2356
Shares many features with Oddbins, specialising in rare and old super-premium Australian wines, but also with an impeccable imported wine list. Excellent monthly newsletter, and the indent club makes imported wine offers monthly, specialising in Bordeaux, Burgundy and Italian wines.

Vintage Cellars

Cnr Wyvern Ave & Pacific Hwy, Chatswood North
phone (02) 9419 5426 **fax** (02) 9419 2790
398 New South Head Road, Double Bay
phone (02) 9327 1333 **fax** (02) 9327 1336
Both carry the complete range of all Vintage Cellars wines, including the full museum stock of Penfolds Grange available from time to time (mostly acquired from Anders Josephson in 1997). The Double Bay store established a major client base and reputation when known as Quaffers, and continues to be a high profile and very successful super-premium wine store.

victoria

Bedelis Liquor Emporium

33 Centreway, Mount Waverley
phone (03) 9802 7033 **fax** (03) 9887 9707
Chris Bedelis is one of the great characters of the Melbourne wine scene, but runs a high quality business with an emphasis on special tastings and events.

Blackburn Cellars

Cnr Canterbury Road & Lawrence Street, Blackburn South
phone (03) 9877 3696 **fax** (03) 9894 2973

Highly regarded business which has been in operation for 25 years. Prides itself on its friendly service and extensive range of Australian wines.

Dan Murphy Cellars

789 Heidelberg Road, Alphington
phone (03) 9497 3388 **fax** (03) 9497 2782
Dan Murphy, the doyen of wine merchants in Australia, has long combined aggressive pricing with an attractive array of wines across the full range of quality and style. Claims to offer the largest range of wines available at one site in Melbourne, covering all regions and ranging from small boutique wineries to the largest. Also a comprehensive range of imported wines.

King & Godfree

293–297 Lygon Street, Carlton
phone (03) 9347 1619 **fax** (03) 9347 3811
Founded in 1870, and one of the first stores in Melbourne to be granted a liquor licence. Continuous operation at 293 Lygon Street, Carlton, and received the Liquor News Australia Liquor Retailer of the Year Award for 1996. Aims to provide superior personal service and competitive prices to both retail and corporate customers.

Philip Murphy Fine Wines

481 Toorak Road, Toorak
phone (03) 9826 1476 **fax** (03) 9826 1172
The top store of the Philip Murphy fine wine group of retail shops (address for others in the Melbourne phone book) and one of the undoubted pace-setters not only for Melbourne, but for Australia as a whole. Particularly strong in top quality imported wines, but without detracting from a superlative coverage of Australian wines. The prices are always competitive.

Richmond Hill Cellars

132 Bridge Road, Richmond
phone (03) 9428 5171 **fax** (03) 9428 3839
A Melbourne establishment, run by the irrepressible Judy Farrow, and which has been in (very successful) business for 20 years. Monthly newsletter always offers an eclectic selection of wines with well written

tasting notes. Offerings range from high quality imports to small Australian wineries seldom offered elsewhere.

Templestowe Cellars

132 James Street, Templestowe
phone (03) 9846 1985 **fax** (03) 9846 5568
The untimely death of Melbourne identity Spiro Karavedes in 1997 has not affected the thriving business of Templestowe Cellars serving the wealthy eastern suburbs of Melbourne. An excellent array of fine wines, always well priced, and always well chosen.

The de Burgh-Day Wine Company

Building 38 Lionel Street, Essendon Airport
phone (03) 5426 4188 **fax** (03) 5426 4472
A retailer without a conventional retail shop, acting as a self-importer and direct seller (via mail list) of an exotic array of imported wines.

Vintage Cellars

254 Coventry Street, South Melbourne
phone (03) 9645 7150 **fax** (03) 9645 7172
620 Hampton Street, Brighton East
phone (03) 9592 4321
The two Melbourne super-stores, offering the entire Vintage Cellars range including all museum stocks of Grange.

south australia

Baily & Baily

537 Portrush Road, Glenunga
phone (08) 88379 0299 **fax** (08) 8379 0113 **email** baily@mpx.com.au,
internet http://www.auswine.com.au
A fine wine retailer with a thriving Australia-wide business thanks to the extraordinary range of imported wines, keen pricing and a truly excellent newsletter. Draws on many sources for its imported wines, and is not afraid to step into the esoteric. Strong list of premium and super-premium Australian wines, including some very interesting back vintages.

Edinburgh Cellars

7 High Street, Mitcham
phone (08) 8373 2753 **fax** (08) 8271 8904
A landmark institution in Adelaide, energetically offering an immaculately selected range of wines. Special wine and food tasting events regularly organised through the year are a special feature. Two-level extensions to the building were opened in late November 1997, featuring a tasting area suitable for wine club functions, tutored tastings, exhibitions and small specialist dinners.

Melbourne Street Cellars

93 Melbourne Street, North Adelaide
phone (08) 8267 1533 **fax** (08) 8267 1772
Established in the mid-1960s, and owned by John and Terry Swanson since 1987, Melbourne Street Cellars stocks around 3000 lines, predominantly wine, but no wine is listed without a rigid tasting process with notes taken regarding value, quality, competition and so forth. Public tastings are conducted every Thursday night 5 pm to 8 pm and Saturday 11 a.m. to 5 p.m.

Super Cellars Parkside

74 Glen Osmond Road, Parkside
phone (08) 8272 9796 **fax** (08) 8272 9796
Energetic retailer with a strong selection of back vintages of the great classics as well as an extensive range of current release wines. Public wine tastings held every Friday and Saturday, and a wine club meeting every six weeks.

Vintage Cellars

Walkerville Cellars
89 Walkerville Terrace, Walkerville
phone (08) 8344 5691 **fax** (08) 8344 6471
A quite amazing business, which throughout the 1960s, '70s and '80s was one of Australia's foremost importers of French and German wine, with mouthwateringly low prices. Because of this huge reputation, continues to trade as Walkerville Cellars, even though it is part of the Vintage Cellars group.

western australia

Cellared Wines

49 Guildford Road, Mt Lawley
phone (08) 9271 1047 **fax** (08) 9271 1714
Prides itself on having one of the largest ranges of premium and hard-to-get wines in Perth, not surprisingly with a strong representation of Western Australian wines. Regular tastings are held.

Chateau Guildford

124 Swan Street, Guildford
phone (08) 9377 3311 **fax** (08) 9377 3611
Chateau Guildford carries an extensive range of wines from around Australia and around the world. Sources of special interest include innovative winemakers from Australia, Burgundy, the Rhône Valley, Bordeaux, Italy and the United States. Owner Alan Dinneen organises regular tastings and issues a periodic newsletter to interested clients.

John Coppins

502 Stirling Hwy, Perth
phone (08) 9384 0777 **fax** (08) 9383 2452
Known throughout Australia thanks to the near-fanaticism of John Jens. Single-minded pursuit of quality, particularly of imported wines, but also Australian. A huge knowledge of the wine styles of the world is reflected in the advice given to all customers.

Scarborough Cellars

166 Scarborough Beach Road, Scarborough
phone (08) 9341 1437
Established in 1977 by Kevin Lukey, who continues to personally manage the business as cellar master. Specialist in French Champagne and in wine education, with regular tastings, an annual wine journal, free mailing list and friendly advice.

Vintage Cellars

95 Nicholson Road, Shenton Park
phone (08) 9381 6555 **fax** (08) 9381 6367

The leading Vintage Cellars store for the west, with the full range of wines, including — of course — the museum collection of Penfolds Grange.

queensland

McGuires Cellars Paddington Tavern

181 Given Terrace, Paddington
phone (07) 3217 5093, **freecall** 1800 069 790 **fax** (07) 3369 7064
Claims to have one of the largest selections of wines in Queensland at competitive prices, and prides itself on extensive staff training in wine and food matching. Issues a regular newsletter with industry news, fine wine specials and details of wine tasting functions.

The Gap Tavern

21 Glenquarie Place, The Gap
phone (07) 3366 6090
The Gap Tavern stocks a wide range of wines at competitive prices; offers wine tastings, a regular newsletter and a home delivery service.

The Grape

Wickham Hotel
308 Wickham Street, Fortitude Valley
phone (07) 3852 1618
Carindale Hotel
The Homemaker Centre, Carindale Street, Carindale
phone (07) 3843 0112
John Kelly and consultant Tony Harper have established themselves as Brisbane's leading fine wine retailers, with excellently laid out stores, informative newsletters, an active tasting and promotional programme, and, above all else, a marvellous selection of Australian and imported wines.

langton's classification of distinguished australian wine

Reproduced from the *Australian Fine Wine Investment Guide 1998* with the kind permission of Langton's Fine Wine Auctions and G & O Publishing Partners.

Outstanding (A)

Penfolds Grange Bin 95 Shiraz, South Australia
Henschke 'Hill of Grace' Keyneton Shiraz, South Australia
Mount Mary 'Quintet' Yarra Valley Cabernets, Victoria

Outstanding

Brokenwood 'Graveyard Vineyard' Hunter Valley Shiraz, New South Wales
Henschke 'Cyril Henschke' Cabernet Sauvignon, South Australia
Henschke 'Mount Edelstone' Keyneton Shiraz, South Australia
Leeuwin Estate 'Art Series' Margaret River Chardonnay, Western Australia
Moss Wood Margaret River Cabernet Sauvignon, Western Australia
Mount Mary Yarra Valley Pinot Noir, Victoria
Penfolds Bin 707 Cabernet Sauvignon, South Australia
Petaluma Piccadilly Valley Chardonnay, South Australia
Petaluma Coonawarra, South Australia
Tyrrells Vat 47 Hunter Valley Chardonnay, New South Wales
Wynns Coonawarra Estate 'John Riddoch' Cabernet Sauvignon, South Australia
Yarra Yering 'Dry Red No. 1' Yarra Valley Cabernet, Victoria

Excellent (A)

Bannockburn Geelong Pinot Noir, Victoria
Cape Mentelle Margaret River Cabernet Sauvignon, Western Australia
Craiglee Sunbury Shiraz, Victoria
Cullen Margaret River Cabernet–Merlot, Western Australia

De Bortoli 'Noble One' Griffith Botrytis Semillon, New South Wales
Jasper Hill 'Emily's Paddock' Heathcote Shiraz-Cabernet Franc, Victoria
Jim Barry 'The Armagh' Clare Valley Shiraz, South Australia
Lake's Folly Hunter Valley Cabernets, New South Wales
Mount Mary Yarra Valley Chardonnay, Victoria
Penfolds 'St Henri' Shiraz, South Australia
Petaluma Clare Valley Riesling, South Australia
Pipers Brook Vineyard Chardonnay, Tasmania
Redbank 'Sally's Paddock' Dry Red, Victoria
Tyrrell's Vat 1 Hunter Valley Semillon, New South Wales
Virgin Hills Kyneton Dry Red, Victoria
Wolf Blass 'Black Label' Dry Red, Area Blend
Yarra Yering Yarra Valley Pinot Noir, Victoria
Yarra Yering 'Dry Red No. 2' Yarra Valley Shiraz, Victoria
Yeringberg Yarra Valley Cabernet, Victoria

Excellent

Bannockburn Geelong Chardonnay, Victoria
Bowen Estate Coonawarra Cabernet Sauvignon, South Australia
Chateau Reynella McLaren Vale Vintage Port, South Australia
Chateau Tahbilk Goulburn Valley Shiraz 1860 Vines, Victoria
Coldstream Hills 'Reserve' Yarra Valley Chardonnay, Victoria
Dalwhinnie Moonambel Cabernet, Victoria
Dalwhinnie Moonambel Shiraz, Victoria
Grosset 'Polish Hill' Clare Valley Riesling, South Australia
Grosset 'Watervale' Clare Valley Riesling, South Australia
Hardys 'Eileen Hardy' Shiraz, South Australia
Hardys McLaren Vale Vintage Port, South Australia
Jasper Hill 'Georgia's Paddock' Heathcote Shiraz, Victoria
Lake's Folly Hunter Valley Chardonnay, New south Wales
Leconfield Coonawarra Cabernet, South Australia
Lindemans 'Limestone Ridge Vineyard' Coonawarra Shiraz-Cabernet, South Australia
Lindemans 'Pyrus' Coonawarra Cabernet, South Australia
Lindemans 'St. George Vineyard' Coonawarra Cabernet Sauvignon, South Australia
Mountadam Eden Valley Chardonnay, South Australia
Orlando 'St. Hugo' Coonawarra Cabernet Sauvignon, South Australia
Penfolds 'Magill Estate' Magill Vineyard Shiraz, South Australia
Penfolds Bin 389 Cabernet-Shiraz, South Australia
Pierro Margaret River Chardonnay, Western Australia
Pipers Brook Vineyard Riesling, Tasmania
Rosemount 'Show Reserve' Hunter Valley Chardonnay, New South Wales
St. Hallett 'Old Block Shiraz' Barossa Valley, South Australia
Wendouree Clare Valley Cabernet-Malbec, South Australia
Wendouree Clare Valley Cabernet Sauvignon, South Australia
Wendouree Clare Valley Shiraz, South Australia
Wynns Coonawarra Estate Cabernet Sauvignon, South Australia

Price Realisations in 1997

Description	1994	1993	1992	1991	1990	1989	1988	1987	1986	1985	1984
Penfolds Grange, Shiraz	–	–	210–210	230–290	410–440	180–210	170–230	130–175	300–350	200–220	180–220
Henschke 'Hill of Grace'	–	–	130–180	170–200	260–270	140–180	180–220	120–140	240–270	150–170	160–180
Mount Mary 'Quintet'	80–100	65–80	75–95	75–95	100–150	85–100	85–100	85–100	130–150	95–130	100–130
Brokenwood 'Graveyard' Shiraz	40–60	40–60	56–68	65–75	42–48	45–55	50–60	50–61	66–72	44–48	38–40
Henschke 'Cyril Henschke'	–	80–95	70–75	60–80	110–128	50–60	50–60	50–60	75–95	50–60	44–54
Henschke 'Mount Edelstone'	–	55–60	50–60	60–75	60–75	55–65	55–65	55–65	75–95	50–56	–
Leeuwin Estate Chardonnay	38–48	38–48	55–65	60–70	70–85	50–55	60–70	100–120	55–65	55–65	60–70
Moss Wood Cabernet	50–60	55–65	50–60	60–70	70–80	60–70	62–71	80–90	80–90	65–66	55–64
Mount Mary Pinot Noir	52–57	50–55	54–58	55–61	60–70	63–66	55–59	54–62	65–76	71–82	60–66
Penfolds Bin 707 Cabernet	60–70	65–75	60–65	85–90	90–110	60–70	75–95	80–85	90–100	69–85	65–80
Petaluma Chardonnay	28–31	30–36	40–47	33–36	40–50	30–40	35–41	39–43	30–35	–	–
Petaluma Coonawarra	30–38	30–40	35–38	30–36	40–44	Not made	34–43	32–36	46–53	32–40	30–41
Tyrrells Vat 47	25–30	26–32	24–29	31–38	26–31	34–36	31–35	40–44	35–40	30–40	35–40
Wynns 'John Riddoch'	–	40–42	38–45	50–56	70–90	Not made	40–46	56–65	75–90	60–70	53–65
Yarra Yering 'Dry Red No. 1'	–	55–62	52–60	55–65	70–85	40–46	38–47	38–59	80–90	40–60	48–50
Bannockburn Pinot Noir	32–36	30–35	38–45	30–34	30–36	–	34–37	36–38	34–38	30–32	30–40
Cape Mentelle Cabernet	–	–	–	40–48	40–45	38–42	40–45	41–42	44–47	36–45	40–55
Craiglee Shiraz	26–30	28–32	30–34	32–36	45–52	–	30–36	30–40	40–50	36–40	–
Cullen Cabernet–Merlot	40–46	34–38	44–48	46–50	44–48	32–38	35–40	45–51	41–42	–	–
De Bortoli 'Noble One'	–	32–36	30–36	30–40	30–40	–	38–42	40–42	34–38	50–52	55–60
Jasper Hill 'Emily's Paddock'	54–60	50–60	55–62	50–54	50–65	50–55	50–55	–	50–70	–	–
Jim Barry 'The Armagh'	–	100–120	110–123	100–120	110–126	70–95	100–110	80–91	–	95–100	–
Lake's Folly Cabernet	30–35	40–45	30–40	38–39	35–38	40–41	34–38	40–46	42–48	50–60	30–34
Mount Mary Chardonnay	–	34–40	–	46–50	45–51	39–40	43–51	42–46	50–51	48–54	28–34
Penfolds St Henri	–	–	26–33	35–40	44–52	36–42	34–41	42–52	50–60	38–47	44–48
Petaluma Riesling	–	22–24	22–26	24–30	24–30	28–32	34–36	29–32	30–36	–	30–34
Pipers Brook Chardonnay	24–30	28–32	20–24	23–28	32–38	23–30	40–42	44–47	40–42	–	–
Redbank 'Sally's Paddock'	–	32–40	30–40	34–40	30–40	32–44	34–39	20–30	44–48	40–50	40–44
Tyrrell's Vat 1	25–30	24–27	17–22	24–30	20–28	40–46	27–30	27–34	36–44	20–30	24–32
Virgin Hills Dry Red	–	–	26–30	25–30	30–34	Not made	30–36	30–40	34–40	32–36	22–30
Wolf Blass 'Black Label'	–	–	50–60	54–60	60–70	54–58	50–60	55–60	56–65	56–65	50–60
Yarra Yering Pinot Noir	–	–	–	40–50	42–48	35–45	–	44–48	42–47	45–50	44–46

langton's classification of distinguished australian wine

Description	1994	1993	1992	1991	1990	1989	1988	1987	1986	1985	1984
Yarra Yering 'Dry Red No. 2'	–	38–45	40–46	35–40	60–85	–	–	40–60	40–44	40–44	47–50
Yeringberg Cabernet	32–37	35–42	37–40	37–41	55–66	36–42	40–50	40–50	40–50	40–50	46–54
Bannockburn Chardonnay	35–40	35–40	33–35	30–40	30–40	–	–	30–40	34–40	–	–
Bowen Estate Cabernet	24–28	23–27	23–28	26–28	30–36	30–34	25–32	25–30	30–38	28–36	36–40
Chateau Reynella Vintage Port	–	–	–	–	–	–	–	–	–	–	–
Chateau Tahbilk 1860 Vines	–	–	44–60	40–50	50–60	36–46	40–44	35–45	50–65	55–70	43–47
Coldstream 'Reserve' Chardonnay	40–44	30–36	32–34	30–40	28–31	30–40	–	–	–	–	–
Dalwhinnie Cabernet	–	32–38	30–34	32–38	35–40	–	34–38	26–32	38–44	40–46	–
Dalwhinnie Shiraz	34–38	42–45	40–50	45–55	52–60	–	46–54	35–45	38–48	47–56	44–56
Grosset 'Polish Hill' Riesling	23–30	32–38	25–30	–	–	26–36	32–36	–	42–48	32–37	–
Grosset 'Watervale' Riesling	20–25	20–25	20–24	–	–	24–30	–	–	32–34	–	
Hardys 'Eileen Hardy' Shiraz	–	33–40	34–38	45–50	46–52	–	48–52	50–55	–	–	–
Hardys Vintage Port	–	–	–	–	–	–	–	–	–	–	–
Jasper Hill 'Georgia's Paddock'	39–42	40–44	38–42	41–48	40–50	34–42	40–50	Friends 47	40–50	42–48	–
Lake's Folly Chardonnay	30–40	35–40	35–40	–	–	36–38	34–40	38–42	34–40	30–34	24–30
Leconfield Cabernet	24–29	20–26	26–32	25–30	30–35	22–26	26–32	–	25–30	–	32–36
Lindemans 'Limestone Ridge'	–	–	37–42	34–35	37–40	24–28	36–40	25–30	45–50	30–35	27–34
Lindemans 'Pyrus'	–	–	30–40	27–28	27–30	–	26–36	34–38	34–38	34–45	Not made
Lindemans 'St. George'	–	–	26–34	27–30	30–36	22–28	28–36	26–32	41–42	30–40	30–34
Mountadam Chardonnay	–	30–35	34–38	34–40	35–45	26–32	28–38	32–40	28–34	–	–
Orlando 'St. Hugo'	–	–	20–30	23–31	32–41	30–32	34–42	24–28	36–42	–	35–42
Penfolds 'Magill Estate'	–	–	29–32	38–42	42–44	34–38	38–42	38–42	45–56	35–43	17–30
Penfolds Bin 389	–	20–24	20–24	26–34	38–48	24–26	32–38	32–36	44–48	34–37	29–32
Pierro Chardonnay	46–60	37–43	45–48	–	60–70	57–65	50–60	–	–	–	–
Pipers Brook Riesling	20–24	–	–	24–28	23–29	20–24	20–26	24–28	–	–	–
Rosemount 'Show' Chardonnay	–	25–30	24–32	24–26	–	24–28	–	29–34	–	38–42	–
St. Hallett 'Old Block Shiraz'	–	40–50	35–45	36–44	45–53	28–32	31–38	30–40	–	–	–
Wendouree Cabernet–Malbec	–	40–46	40–50	40–50	–	34–40	–	38–44	–	44–60	44–60
Wendouree Cabernet	–	40–50	40–50	40–50	–	–	–	45–52	–	44–60	44–60
Wendouree Shiraz	–	44–50	44–50	50–60	–	–	42–54	48–54	–	50–54	–
Wynns Coonawarra Cabernet Sauvignon	–	15–17	15–18	20–24	30–36	18–24	22–27	18–22	34–70	–	22–25

glossary

Acetaldehyde: The principal aldehyde of wine, occurring in amounts of up to about 100 parts per million.

Acetic acid: A volatile acid present in virtually all table wines in small quantities. The legal limit is 1.2 grams per litre; the flavour threshold is around 0.5 to 0.6 grams per litre. A wine described as volatile suffers from an excess of acetic acid.

Acid: A generic term used to denote the three principal acids present in wine — tartaric, malic and citric. In dry table wine the levels usually fall between 5.5 and 7 grams per litre. Acid plays an essential role in preventing bacterial spoilage, providing longevity and giving flavour balance.

Aggressive: An unpleasantly obvious component of wine flavour, for example, aggressive tannin.

Albillo: An incorrect name for the grape variety chenin blanc.

Alcohol: One of the principal components of wine and derived from the action of yeast on grape sugar during the fermentation process. Most table wines have between 10 and 14 degrees of alcohol; if all of the available grape sugar is fermented, each degree baumé of sugar will produce one degree of alcohol.

Aldehyde: A volatile fluid deriving from the oxidation of alcohol, present in most wines but undesirable in any appreciable quantity; hence, aldehydic.

Aleatico: A grape of the muscat family from Italy and grown in Australia chiefly in the Mudgee region. Produces red or fortified wine of modest quality.

Alicante bouschet (or bouchet): A French hybrid red grape grown extensively in France and, to a lesser degree, California. High-yielding but inferior quality grapes are produced. Limited plantings in Australia, chiefly north-east Victoria.

Alvarelháo: A Portuguese grape variety once propagated in tiny quantities in southern New South Wales and northern Victoria.

Amontillado: A wood-matured sherry, slightly fuller in body and slightly sweeter than fino sherry.

Amoroso: A very old, fully sweet wood-matured sherry. Similar in weight and style to a fortified muscat or tokay.

Ampelography: The science of the identification and classification of grape vines.

Anthocyanin: A colouring pigment which is a form of tannin found in grape skins and which plays an important part in both the colour and keeping qualities of a red wine.

Appellation controlée: A system of laws which guarantees the authenticity of a wine with a given label, extending both to region, grape variety, methods of viticulture and (occasionally) methods of vinification.

Armpit: A colloquial term used to describe the rather sweaty and stuffy smell of a wine which is showing the after-effects of a highly controlled fermentation and maturation in which oxygen has been rigorously excluded. It is a condition which usually passes after the wine has spent a year or so in bottle. For some reason, sauvignon blanc seems to suffer particularly from the character.

Aroma: The scent or smell of the grape variety; aroma decreases with age as bouquet builds.

Astringent; astringency: Sharpness or bitterness deriving usually from tannin and sometimes from acid; particularly evident in a young wine, and can be an indication of the keeping potential of such a wine. Can also be associated with mercaptan, and overall is not a desirable characteristic.

Aubun: An extremely rare red-grape variety from the Mediterranean region of France: a few vines still exist at Best's Great Western Vineyards.

Aucerot: Incorrect name for montils.

Auslese: In Australian usage, a sweet white wine made from late-harvested grapes, often affected by botrytis. Its use is due to be phased out by agreement with the EC.

Autolysis; autolysed: The breakdown of internal barriers within dead cells to allow enzymes present in those cells to digest components of the cell, producing both flavour and structure changes in the wine; a marmite-toast flavour is often noted, while the surface tension of the wine is decreased, leading to smaller bubbles in the sparkling wine in which the process of autolysis occurs.

Backbone: A term used to describe a wine with a core of strength, which derives from acid (in the case of white wine) or from tannin and/or acid (in the case of red wine).

Back palate: The point in the tasting cycle shortly before or shortly after the wine is swallowed.

Balance: The harmony or equilibrium between the different flavour components of wine, and the first requirement of a great wine.

Barbera: The principal red-wine grape of Italy, grown in tiny quantities in Australia, chiefly in Mudgee but also in the Griffith/Riverina. Noted for its high acidity and low pH.

Barrel fermentation: The practice of conducting the primary fermentation in the small oak barrels in which wine is normally stored at the end of fermentation; a common practice in making French white burgundy, but of relatively recent introduction in Australia.

Barrique: An oak barrel containing 225 litres of wine, used almost exclusively in Burgundy and Bordeaux in France for maturation of wine, and increasingly used throughout Australia.

Bastardo: A red-grape variety from Spain incorrectly called cabernet gros in South Australia. Of minor importance.

Baumé: A scale for the measurement of grape sugar. One degree baumé equals 1.8 per cent sugar, or 1.8 degrees brix. (See also **Alcohol**.)

Beerenauslese: As with auslese, the term has no precise meaning in Australia. Adopted from the German, and applied to heavily botrytised, extremely sweet white table wine.

Biancone: A white grape of Corsica, the highest-yielding variety in commercial propagation in Australia. Relatively small plantings in South Australia's Riverland.

Big: Used to describe a wine with above-average flavour, body and/or alcohol. By no means necessarily a favourable description.

Bitter: A fault detectable at the back of the palate, usually deriving from skin, pip or stalk tannins.

Blanquette: Synonym for clairette.

Blue imperial: Synonym for cinsaut.

Body: A term used to describe the weight or substance of a wine in the mouth and deriving from alcohol and tannin. Softens and mellows with age.

Bonvedro: A red grape of Portugal, grown principally in South Australia with a little in New South Wales and Victoria. Produces a relatively light-bodied wine; not an important variety.

Botrytis: *Botrytis cinerea* (called *pourriture noble* in France and *Edelfaule* in Germany) is a microscopic fungus or mould that attacks first the skin and then the pulp of grapes in certain very specific climatic conditions, causing the pulp to lose its water and the grape to soften and shrink with a corresponding concentration of the remaining components of the grape, notably sugar and acid. The grey-brown grapes look extremely unattractive, and the juice first pressed from them equally so, but juice settling and subsequent fermentation produces the great sweet wines of the world. Such wines are usually very long-lived.

Botrytised: Grapes or wine affected by botrytis.

Bottle–development: A reference to the secondary characters and flavours which develop after a wine has been cellared for some years.

Bouquet: The smell of the wine (as opposed to simply the aroma of the grape) produced by the volatile esters present in any wine. Bouquet becomes more complex during the time the wine needs to reach full maturity and finally softens and dissipates with extreme age. Much work still remains to be done to understand fully the very complex chemical changes which take place in a wine as it matures and which contribute to the changing bouquet.

Bourboulenc: A white–grape variety from the Mediterranean region of France. Imported in 1832 but now restricted to a few vines in central and northern Victoria. Unlikely ever to be of significance in Australia.

Bready: Literally the smell of freshly baked bread, often associated with the influence of yeast, and probably, but by no means necessarily, a pleasant aroma.

Breathing: The process of allowing a wine to come in contact with air by drawing the cork (and possibly decanting) prior to serving.

Enhances the development of the bouquet. The optimum period of time is frequently the subject of fierce debate among experts, but one or two hours is a safe estimate for young or semi-mature wines.

Brix degrees: An alternative measure of the approximate sugar content of wine; most grapes are harvested between 19 and 24 brix. One degree brix produces one degree proof spirit.

Broad: A term used to describe wine which is softly coarse, lacking in refinement.

Brown frontignac: Incorrect name for muscat à petite grains.

Brown muscat: Incorrect name for muscat à petite grains.

Brut: The driest of the sparkling-wine styles though in fact containing some sugar.

Bung: The wooden or silicon-rubber stopper in a wine barrel.

Buttery: A term encompassing the aroma, taste and texture of a white wine, usually oak-matured, but which can also develop from long bottle-age. Typically found in semillon and chardonnay.

Cabernet: In Australia, simply an abbreviation for cabernet sauvignon; also used to denote the cabernet family (see below).

Cabernet franc: An important red-grape variety in Bordeaux and the Loire Valley in France; also extensively propagated in Italy. Until recently, little attention was paid to the variety in Australia but it is now assuming greater importance for top-quality reds. Produces a wine similar to but slightly softer than cabernet sauvignon.

Cabernet gros: Incorrect name for bastardo.

Cabernet sauvignon: The great red grape of Bordeaux and, with pinot noir, one of the two most noble red varieties in the world. It has become the most important top-quality red-wine grape in Australia only during the last two decades; prior to that time it was grown in small quantities. Produces the longest-lived of all red wines.

Camphor: A smell which can develop after a wine has spent a number of years in bottle; usually quite pleasant unless it becomes too marked.

Capsule: The lead or plastic covering of the top of the bottle which serves a largely ornamental purpose, and the top of which should always be removed prior to pulling the cork.

Caramel: Literally, a caramel flavour found in wine, usually white wine, and often indicating either oxidation or over-ripe fruit.

Carbonic maceration: A winemaking method which involves a substantial proportion of the primary fermentation taking place within whole berries, which have not been crushed in the usual method. It results in very soft wines with a distinctive aroma of spice and well-hung meat.

Carignan, carignane: A grape variety of Spanish origin but very widely propagated in the south of France to produce *vin ordinaire*. Also extensively grown in California for similar purposes. Some South Australian plantings of an unidentified grape are incorrectly called carignane; the grape is not commercially propagated in Australia.

Cassis: A dark purple liqueur made from blackcurrants, chiefly near Dijon in Burgundy. The aroma of cassis is often found in high-quality cabernet sauvignon as the smell of sweet blackcurrants.

Cedar; cedary: An oak-derived aroma or taste reminiscent of the smell of cedar, usually developed in older red wines.

Cépage: A French word for grape variety, but increasingly used to denote the varietal composition of a wine made from a blend of several varieties (hence, *cépagement)*.

Chalky: A rather dry, dusty aroma or taste, often found in young wines made from chenin blanc in the Loire Valley of France; may also be due to solids fermentation (see hereunder).

Chaptalisation: The addition of sugar to partly fermented wine to increase the alcohol level, permitted in France but illegal in Australia.

Character: The overall result of the combination of vinosity, balance and style of wine.

Chardonnay: The greatest white grape of France (Burgundy and Champagne), grown extensively throughout the world and in particular in California. All but unknown in Australia before 1970, it has had a meteoric rise since. As elsewhere, it provides rich table wines and fine sparkling wines. In Australia and California the wines have tended to develop quickly; in France they improve over and live for a far longer period of time.

Charred oak: A particular taste deriving from oak which has been deliberately charred during the heating process needed to shape the wooden staves into barrel form. A complex, pleasantly smoky/toasty aroma and flavour is often the result.

Chasselas: The principal white wine grape of Switzerland, and also extensively propagated in France and Italy. In Europe and Australia it is used both for winemaking and as a table grape. In the last century it was called sweet-water: the principal area of propagation in Australia is at Great Western in Victoria.

Cheesy: A smell (and very occasionally a taste) which principally occurs in white wines and which tends to diminish fruit aromas. Its most likely cause is a degree of oxidation or perhaps yeast problems. Not particularly desirable.

Chenin blanc: The principal white grape of the Loire Valley in France, grown in relatively small quantities in Western Australia, South Australia and Victoria and for long incorrectly identified variously as semillon and albillo. Seldom produces wines of the same character as in the Loire Valley, but the plantings have recently shown a modest increase. Can produce great botrytised wines.

Chewy: A term used to denote the structure (rather than the flavour) of a wine which just stops short of being thick or heavy; generally a term of qualified approval.

Cigar-box: Literally the smell of an empty cigar-box, usually manifesting itself in older red wines and deriving from oak. Sometimes present in young wines. Usually a term of approbation.

Cinsaut: A red-grape variety from the Mediterranean region of France. Frequently called blue imperial in north-east Victoria, black prince at Great Western and confused with oeillade in South Australia. Produces agreeable soft wines with good colour but low in tannin which age quickly.

Clairette: A once very important white-grape variety in the south of France, grown in relatively small quantities in Australia where it is often called blanquette (particularly in the Hunter Valley). A difficult wine to make and of no great merit.

Clare riesling: Incorrect name for crouchen.

Classic: A wine conforming exactly to style and of the highest quality.

Classified growth: A wine formally recognised and classified under one of the French quality-grading systems, the best known being the 1855 classification of the great wines of Bordeaux into five growths (or *crus*).

Clean: The absence of any foreign (or 'off') odour or flavour; an important aspect of a wine of quality.

Closed: A wine lacking fruit aroma and possibly flavour; normally affects young wines and diminishes with age.

Cloudy: Colloidal haze and gas particulate matter in suspension leading to a hazy or milky appearance.

Cloying: A sweet wine without sufficient balancing acid.

Coarse: Indicates a wine with excessive extract of solids, particularly tannins, and probably affected by oxidation during the making process.

Coffee: An undesirable taste or aroma reminiscent of coffee, normally indicating oxidation.

Colombard: A white grape extensively grown in France, used both for table-wine making and also in the production of brandy. Extensively propagated in California where it is known as French colombard. Has been planted extensively in Australia's warm irrigated regions because of its excellent acid-retention capacity. Used both in blends and in varietal white wines, but does not aspire to any great quality or longevity.

Complete: Denotes a wine which has all of the requisite flavours and components in harmony and balance.

Complex: A term of commendation, but otherwise having its normal English meaning.

Condition: A technical term to describe the clarity of a wine; a cloudy wine is described as being out of condition.

Corked; corkiness: Refers to a wine affected by microscopic moulds (chiefly of the penicillin family) which penetrate corks in the cork factory and which subsequently impart a sour, mouldy taste in the wine.

Cosmetic: A somewhat imprecise term used to indicate a foreign, and often faintly sickly, aroma (or possibly flavour).

Coulure: A disease leading to the flowers or immature berries falling from the vine with a consequent reduction in crop level.

Creamy: A term used particularly in relation to sparkling wine and intended to denote texture more than flavour.

Crisp: A term of commendation, but otherwise having its normal English meaning.

Crouchen: A white grape originally from France but now propagated only in South Africa and Australia. The substantial plantings in this country have been consistently incorrectly identified for a century, being called Clare riesling in the Clare Valley, semillon in the Barossa Valley, and firstly Clare riesling and then semillon in South Australia's Riverland, before being finally identified as crouchen. A relatively high-yielding variety, producing wines of modest quality; of declining importance.

Crusher: A machine to remove the berries from the stalks prior to fermentation, forming a must which will be pressed shortly thereafter if it is a white wine, and pressed at the end of fermentation if it is a red wine.

Crust: Sediment adhering to the inside of bottles of wine, usually red: consists mainly of pigment and tartrate crystals.

Decant: The careful pouring of the contents of a bottle into a carafe or decanter to leave behind the crust or other deposits.

Deep: Indicates both complexity and profundity when applied to aroma; indicates depth (or intensity) of hue when applied to colour.

Developed: Showing the effects of ageing in bottle, usually but not invariably beneficially so.

Dolcetto: A red grape from Piedmont in Italy, grown in tiny quantities in South Australia and Victoria. Many of the old classic Saltram reds contained small quantities of the variety.

Doradillo: An extremely important white grape in Australia but of little significance elsewhere. Brought to Australia from Spain. Grown principally in the Riverland for distillation into brandy and for the production of sherry.

Downy mildew: One of the two principal vine fungi, which can be devastating if not checked.

Drive: A mining term used to denote a horizontal extension of a mine shaft.

Dry: A wine without apparent sweetness or residual sugar; in fact many wines contain minute traces of sugar, and it is difficult to detect at levels of up to five grams per litre.

Dull: Denotes a wine either cloudy or hazy in colour, or with a muted or flawed bouquet or palate.

Dumb: A wine showing either no aroma or distinct varietal taste or no development.

Durif: A variety first propagated in the Rhône Valley only a century ago, and called petite sirah in California. Grown in tiny amounts in Australia, notably in north-eastern Victoria by Morris, where it produces a robust full-bodied style.

Dusty: Used to describe both the bouquet and taste of red wine, and normally denoting a character caused by long storage in big, old (but sound) oak casks.

Earthy: Bouquet and flavour reminiscent of certain soil types; a smell of fresh earth can often be identified in young vintage port.

Esparte: Synonym for mourvedre.

Esters: Flavourful and usually volatile substances formed by the combination of acids with alcohols. Wine probably contains over 100 different esters.

Extract: Soluble solids adding to the body and substance of a wine.

Extractive: A coarse wine with excessive extract from skins and pips.

Fading: A wine past its peak, losing its bouquet, flavour and character.

Farana: A white grape from the Mediterranean region grown in tiny quantities in the Barossa Valley, where it was previously confused with trebbiano. Orlando briefly experimented with varietal bottlings in the 1970s.

Fermentation: The primary winemaking process in which the sugar (in the form of glucose and fructose) in grapes is converted to alcohol and carbon dioxide by the action of yeasts.

Ferruginous: A wine tasting of iron, possibly derived from the soil type.

Fetayaska: A white grape grown in tiny quantities in north-east Victoria and South Australia to make a white table wine of no great significance.

Filter pad: A synthetic woven sheet used to remove suspended solids and bacteria from wine. Incorrect treatment may lead to a particular cardboard-like taste being imparted to the wine, often referred to as paddy.

Finesse: A term denoting a wine of high quality and style.

Fining: A method of clarifying young wines before bottling by the addition of beaten egg white, bentonite or other fining agent.

Finish: The flavour or taste remaining after the wine leaves the mouth.

Fino: A Spanish-derived term for the driest and most delicate type of sherry made by the flor-yeast process.

Firm: A term usually applied to the finish of a wine, and denoting the impact of tannin and possibly acid.

Flabby: A wine without sufficient acid and freshness, often due to excessive age but sometimes to poor winemaking.

Flat: Similar to dull and flabby; a lack of freshness, character, or acid.

Fleshy: A youthful wine with full-bodied varietal flavour.

Flowery: The aroma reminiscent of flowers contributed by certain aromatic grape varieties.

Folle blanche: A still important white-grape variety used in the production of brandy in France. The supposed Australian plantings have now been identified as ondenc.

Fore-palate: Used to describe that part of the tasting cycle as the wine is first taken into the mouth.

Foxy: The unpleasantly cloying, sweet aroma of wines produced from *Vitis labrusca* grapes.

Free-run: Wine that separates without pressing from grape skins after fermentation and which is generally more fruity and lower in tannin than the pressings that follow.

Fresh: An aroma or taste free from any fault or bottle-developed characters, usually found in a young wine but occasionally in old wines.

Frontignac: Incorrect name for muscat à petite grains.

Fruity: The pleasant aromatic taste of a young wine with strong varietal character.

Fumé blanc: A name coined by Robert Mondavi of the Napa Valley to describe a barrel-fermented or oak-matured sauvignon blanc. Now in more general use and may (but does not necessarily) indicate a sauvignon blanc in Australian usage; the term has no legal standing, and it is possible for the wine to be made from any variety, although it should by rights show some oak influence.

Furmint: One of the white grapes used to make the famous Hungarian tokay. A few vines exist at Great Western and one or two boutique wineries have experimental plantings.

Furry: A term used to denote a particular aspect of the texture (rather than the taste) of a red wine, almost invariably deriving from tannin and akin to the sensation of soft fur on the side of the tongue.

Gamay: Gamay is the red grape which produces beaujolais in France;: it is also grown extensively in the Loire Valley. Two attempts to introduce the variety into Australia from California have failed. The first introduction turned out to be pinot noir, the second valdigue. Still grown only in tiny quantities; it seems inevitable that further attempts to propagate it in the future will be made.

Gassy: A wine with small bubbles of carbon dioxide, often mistaken for a form of secondary fermentation. Undesirable (particularly in red wines) but tolerated in Australia.

Generic: A term used to denote a wine falling within a general style (e.g. chablis, white burgundy, claret) and not made from any particular grape variety or from any particular region.

Gewurztraminer: Synonym for traminer.

Glory of Australia: A black grape from the Burgundy region of France, from which it disappeared after phylloxera; frequently mentioned in the nineteenth-century accounts of the vineyards of Geelong. A few vines survive at Great Western. Also called liverdun, la gloire, but correctly called troyen.

Glycerine: A by-product of fermentation which adds to the texture of a white wine. Sometimes (improperly) added to white wine, particularly chardonnay.

Gouais: A minor white-grape variety from the centre of France, extensively propagated in Victoria in the nineteenth century but now largely disappeared except from areas around Rutherglen.

Goût de Lumière: A wine fault in champagne associated with hydrogen sulphide and believed to be caused by the effect of ultra-violet light on bottled wine.

Graciano: A red variety of importance in Spain's Rioja area. Called morrastel in France, but unrelated to the variety once called thus in South Australia (which is in fact mourvedre). Grown in small quantities in northern–eastern Victoria. Produces strongly coloured wines, rich in tannin and extract, which age well.

Grassy; grassiness: Literally the smell of freshly cut or partially dried grass, found very frequently in sauvignon blanc and in cabernet sauvignon grown in cooler areas or in cooler vintages. Can also occur occasionally in other varieties, particularly semillon. Provided it is present in moderation, it is more likely to be desirable than not.

Gravel; gravelly: Denotes a slightly flinty, slightly sour, taste akin to the taste (or sensation) of sucking a pebble.

Green: Term applied to a young wine which is unbalanced because of excess malic acid deriving from unripe grapes.

Green–yellow: The colour of white wine in which green tones predominate over yellow, but both are present. Highly desirable.

Grip: A component of the structure of a wine which probably has marked acid, but usually a term of qualified approval.

Hard: An unbalanced and unyielding wine suffering from an excess of tannin and/or acid (if red) and acid (if white).

Harsh: Usually applied to red wine suffering from excess tannin, often when young.

Hárslevelü: A white grape of Hungary used in making Hungarian tokay. Tiny plantings in Australia.

Herbaceous: Similar to grassy, but indicating a slightly broader spectrum of grass and herb-like flavours, usually a little richer and more complete. As in the case of a grassy wine, should not be excessively marked.

Hermitage: An incorrect name for shiraz.

Hogshead: A barrel of 300 litres capacity, once the most widely used small barrel in Australia but progressively replaced by barriques and puncheons.

Hollow: Applies to a wine with fore-taste and finish, but with no flavour on the middle palate.

Honeyed: Denotes both the flavour and the structure (or feel in the mouth) of a mature white wine, particularly aged semillon but also sauterne.

Horizontal tasting: A tasting of a number of wines made in the same vintage, usually of a single variety or from a single region. The one essential feature is the common vintage.

Hunter River riesling: Incorrect name for semillon.

Hybrid: A cross between an American and a European vine achieved by cross-pollination as opposed to grafting.

Hydrogen sulphide: The smell of rotten eggs found in red wines resulting from the reduction of sulphur dioxide or elemental sulphur. Detectable in tiny quantities (one part per million); when bound into the wine it becomes mercaptan.

Integrated; integration: Used in relation to a wine in which (most probably) fruit and oak flavours have blended harmoniously and merged imperceptibly into each other; a most desirable characteristic.

Intensity: Applied in particular in relation to fruit aroma or flavour; very different from weight; normally used in relation to a high-class wine.

Irvine's white: Incorrect name for ondenc.

Jacquez: An American variety thought to be a naturally occurring hybrid between the species *Vitis aestivalis* and *Vitis vinifera*. Small quantities grown in the Griffith/Riverina area and the Hunter Valley where it is usually called troia. It has a strong, unusual flavour less unpleasant than those of the species *Vitis labrusca*.

Jammy: Excessively ripe and heavy red-grape flavours, sweet but cloying.

Lactic acid: Seldom present in grapes but formed during the alcoholic and malolactic fermentations. Also occurs in faulty wines as a result of bacterial decomposition of sugars: the slightly sickly sourmilk aroma is very unpleasant.

Leafy: Yet another variant of the grassy/herbaceous spectrum of flavours, usually the lightest in weight. May or may not be pleasant.

Leathery: A slightly sour, astringent smell or taste, almost certainly deriving from small concentrations of mercaptan.

Lees: Deposit of bacteria, tartar, yeast and other solids found on the bottom of a vessel containing wine.

Lift; lifted: Usually applied in relation to a wine with a degree of volatility, but in which that volatility is not excessive.

Light: Lack of body, but otherwise pleasant.

Lime: A lime-juice flavour commonly encountered in rhine riesling, and often (but not invariably) indicating that the fruit has been affected by botrytis.

Limousin: A particular type of French oak with a distinctive spicy aroma and taste.

Long: Denotes the capacity of the flavours of the wine to linger in the mouth and palate after the wine has been swallowed.

Madeira:

(i)   Island off the coast of Spain famous for its dessert wines.

(ii) General term for wines resembling those produced on the island.

(iii) Incorrect name for verdelho.

Madeirised: Oxidative change in white wines brought about by prolonged storage in warm conditions.

Malbec: A red-grape variety grown chiefly in and around Bordeaux and also in the Loire Valley where it is known as cot. Grown on a vast scale in Argentina and in a minor way throughout Australia. Has been confused with dolcetto and tinta amarella. Ideal for blending with cabernet sauvignon which it softens and fills out. Seldom released as a straight varietal.

Malic: A rather tart, green flavour deriving from higher than normal levels of malic acid, an acid found in all grapes but usually converted to lactic acid during the secondary fermentation.

Malolactic fermentation: A secondary fermentation, usually taking place after the primary fermentation, involving the decomposition of malic acid in wine to lactic acid and carbon dioxide. Considered essential for most red wines, and increasingly used in the making of wines such as wood-matured chardonnay. Softens and adds complexity to the flavour of wine.

Malty: Literally, the taste of malt; not a particularly desirable wine characteristic.

Mammolo: A red-grape variety once of minor importance in Tuscany, Italy; a few vines exist in Mudgee, and there have apparently been some other isolated recent plantings. The wine is said to have an aroma resembling the scent of violets.

Marc: The residue of grape skins and seeds after the pressing process has been completed; can be distilled into a spirit bearing the same name.

Marsanne: A white-grape variety of declining importance in the Rhône Valley of France, grown in relatively small quantities in the Goulburn Valley, north-east Victoria and the Hunter Valley. Once famous in the Yarra Valley, where tiny plantings also still exist.

Mataro: Incorrect name for mourvedre.

Matchbox: Literally the smell of a box of matches, a slightly sulphurous/wood smell; not at all desirable.

Meaty: The smell of slightly aged, raw meat, usually although not inevitably a form of mercaptan.

Medicinal: A somewhat vague term used to describe childhood recollections of cough mixture; not desirable.

Melon: A white grape which originated in Burgundy but is now propagated principally in the Loire Valley, where it is known as muscadet. Significant plantings in California are called pinot blanc. Only small quantities are propagated in Australia, chiefly in South Australia.

Mercaptan: Produced by ethyl mercaptan and ethyl sulphides in wine deriving from hydrogen sulphide and produced during the fermentation process. It manifests itself in a range of unpleasant odours ranging from burnt rubber to garlic, onion, gamy meat, stale cabbage and asparagus. While hydrogen sulphide can easily be removed, once mercaptan is formed it is much more difficult to eliminate.

Merlot: One of the most important red-grape varieties in the Bordeaux region, dominant in St Emilion and Pomerol. A relatively recent arrival in California, and in Australia, where poor fruit set has caused some problems. However, growers are persevering and plantings are on the increase. Softer and earlier maturing than cabernet sauvignon, with which it is frequently blended.

Metallic: A taste of metal, sometimes encountered in red wines which have been treated with copper sulphate to remove mercaptan.

Methode champenoise: The method of making sparkling wine employed in Champagne in which the all-important second fermentation takes place in the bottle in which the wine is ultimately sold.

Meunier: A red grape almost invariably known under its synonym pinot meunier in Australia. Also called Miller's burgundy at Great Western. A naturally occurring derivative of pinot noir and grown principally in France in Champagne. The upsurge in interest in sparkling wine in Australia may see an increase in the presently small and isolated plantings, chiefly in Victoria.

Mid-palate: The mid-point of the tasting cycle, as the wine rests in the centre of the mouth.

Millerandage: Obviously enough, a French term, which has been colloquially translated as 'hen-and-chicken', a vivid description of bunches containing both full-sized and stunted or unformed berries. The very small berries, if formed at all, carry no seeds as they are unfertilised. The condition is due to wind and/or rain at flowering.

Miller's burgundy: Incorrect name for meunier.

Mint; minty: An aroma and flavour of red wine in the eucalypt/peppermint spectrum, and not garden mint.

Modulated: A wine in which varietal aroma or flavour is very well-balanced between the extremes such aroma or flavour can on occasions take.

Monbadon: A white variety of declining importance in Bordeaux and Cognac; grown on a small scale around the Corowa–Wahgunyah in north-eastern Victoria.

Mondeuse: A red grape of minor importance in the east of France, grown chiefly by Brown Brothers at Milawa in north-eastern Victoria. Produces a very strong tannic wine ideal for blending with softer varieties.

Montils: A white grape grown in small quantities in Cognac. Small plantings in the Hunter Valley where it is also known as aucerot; the aucerot of north-eastern Victoria is a separate and, as yet, unidentified variety. Produces a wine with low pH and high acidity, and would appear to have at least as much potential as colombard, but little commercial interest has so far been demonstrated.

Moschata paradisa: A white-grape variety grown in tiny quantities in Mudgee, but so far its overseas source has not been identified. Australia's most unusual grape.

Mouldy: 'Off' flavours and aromas derived from mouldy grapes or storage in a mouldy cask or from a bad cork.

Mourvedre: A red grape of major importance in Spain, where it is called morastell or monastrell. Once one of Australia's most important red grapes in terms of production, but now declining. Called balzac at Corowa and esparte at Great Western. Yields well and produces a neutrally flavoured but astringent wine which is best blended with other varieties.

Mousse: The bubbles in sparkling wine.

Mousy: A peculiar flat, undesirable taste resulting from bacterial growth in wines, most evident after the wine leaves the mouth. Its precise cause is not yet known.

Mouth–feel: Literally, the feel rather than the taste of the wine in the mouth; a wine with good mouth-feel will be pleasantly round and soft.

Müller–thurgau: A cross, bred by Dr Müller in 1882 and put into commercial propagation in 1920 in Germany; now that country's most important grape. Originally thought to be a riesling-silvaner cross, but now believed to be a cross of two riesling grapes. Propagated in limited quantities in Australia; produces a fairly uninteresting wine. The most important white grape in New Zealand, where it is generally known as riesling sylvaner.

Muscadelle: The white grape which is the third and least important component of the wines of Sauternes. Grown across Australia, and usually known as tokay. The largest plantings are in South Australia, but in north-east Victoria extremely ripe, raisined grapes are used to make the famous fortified tokay of that region. The grape is not used for this purpose anywhere else in the world.

Muscadet: Synonym for melon.

Muscat à petite grains: A grape variety grown over much of Europe and which is called by a wide variety of names both there and in Australia, not surprisingly, given that it appears in three colour variants — white, rose and red. The coloured forms mutate readily from one to the other, while chimeras, in which the genetic make-up of the berry skin differs from that of the flesh, also exist. The white variety is common in South Australia, the red in north-eastern Victoria, where it is known as brown muscat (or brown frontignac) and used to make the great fortified wines of that region. The white variant is used to make table wine of very high flavour, often used in small percentages with other more noble varieties such as rhine riesling. It does not cellar well.

Muscat gordo blanco: A white-grape variety, originating in Spain but grown in many countries. A very important variety in Australia for winemaking and for drying and table-grape use. Widely called muscat of Alexandria, it is a high-yielding multi-purpose grape. For winemaking it is used for fortified sweet wines such as cream sherry and also in cask and flagon wines, often in combination with sultana.

Muscat of Alexandria: Synonym for muscat gordo blanco.

Must: In white-winemaking, unfermented grape juice; in red-winemaking, the mixture of grape juice, skins and seeds before fermentation. During fermentation it is known as fermenting must.

Nevers: An important French oak which imparts a slightly lemony taste, frequently used to mature Cabernet Sauvignon.

Nose: The scents and odours of a wine, encompassing both aroma and bouquet.

Nutty: Characteristic pungent flavour and aroma of sherry, due in part to wood age and to the presence of acetaldehyde.

Oeillade: Incorrect name for cinsaut.

Oenology: The science of winemaking.

Oidium: *Oidium tuckeri,* commonly known as powdery mildew.

Oily: Oils deriving from grape pips or stalks and not desirable in wine.

Olfactory: Pertaining to the sense of smell.

Oloroso: A Spanish term for old, rich, sweet, full-bodied sherry.

Ondenc: An obscure white grape from France, travelling both there and in Australia under a confusingly large number of names. Probably brought to this country in the early nineteenth century as piquepoule, but then became known as sercial in South Australia and Irvine's white in Victoria at Great Western. In France it is used for brandy-making; in Australia for sparkling wine (because of its neutrality), chiefly by Seppelt at Great Western and Drumborg.

Orange muscat: A highly aromatic white-grape variety, also known in France as muscat fleur d'orange, grown chiefly in north-eastern Victoria. Most enjoyable when young and fresh.

Organoleptic: The analytical appreciation, by use of the senses, of wine (or food).

Over-extracted: The term used to describe a wine that is unbalanced and rough (usually too tannic); the winemaker should have removed the wine from its skins earlier in the fermentation process or fermented the wine at lower temperatures. (See **Extractive**.)

Oxidised: Refers to a wine that has been exposed to too much oxygen, resulting in loss of flavour and development of coarseness.

Palomino: A white grape from Spain providing virtually all the raw material for sherry. Grown on a very large scale in South Africa and an important variety in Australia. Very similar to pedro ximinez. Used chiefly for fortified wine in Australia, and in particular dry sherry.

Pastille: The flavour of a fruit pastille, not totally unpleasant but nonetheless undesirable.

Pedro ximinez: Another Spanish variety used to produce both dry and sweet fortified wines. Extensively propagated in Argentina but decreasingly in Australia. Grown chiefly in the Riverland, it is used in the making of sherry, but also to provide flagon and cask white wine.

Peloursin: An ancient grape variety from the east of France but of little or no commercial significance. Survives in Australia and California interplanted with durif, which it resembles.

Pencil shavings: A rather bitter and raw oak aroma or flavour caused by the use of poor oak or unskilled use of oak maturation.

Peppery: May refer to a raw, harsh quality in immature wine, but increasingly recognised as a characteristic of cool-climate shiraz with pepper/spice aromas and flavours.

Petit meslier: An extremely obscure, although still permitted, white-grape variety in Champagne in France; a few vines survive amongst ondenc plantings at Great Western.

Petit verdot: A minor red grape of Bordeaux of declining importance in that region. The once significant Hunter Valley plantings have disappeared since 1930, but a few tiny plantings have since been established elsewhere in Australia by those seeking to emulate the great wines of Bordeaux.

Petite sirah: Incorrect name for durif used throughout America.

pH: Literally, the power of hydrogen. In simple terms it is a logarithmic expression of the measurement of free hydrogen ions in solution. The lower the pH number, the higher the level of hydrogen ions and, in turn, the greater the available or useful acid. Table wine usually has a pH of between 3.1 and 3.6; white wines tend to have a slightly lower pH than reds. Low pH wines will usually age better than those with a higher pH.

Phenolic: Deriving from phenols, important flavour contributors to wine, but denoting a hard or heavy coarse character; not desirable.

Phylloxera: A microscopic insect, introduced into Europe and thence to Australia from America in the second half of the nineteenth century, which devastated the vineyards of Europe and of Victoria. Feeds chiefly by sucking the sap from the roots of the vine.

Pinot blanc: The true pinot blanc is a white variant of pinot noir, seemingly grown only in Alsace, Germany and Italy. Varieties grown elsewhere and called pinot blanc are variously chardonnay, chenin blanc or melon.

Pinot chardonnay: Incorrect name for chardonnay.

Pinot de la Loire: French synonym for chenin blanc.

Pinot gris: Another colour variant of pinot noir similar to pinot blanc. Grown in Alsace, Germany (where it is called rulander) and northern Italy.

Pinot meunier: Synonym for meunier.

Pinot noir: The classic red grape of Burgundy, grown in practically every country in the world but only producing wine of real quality in cool climates. In Australia it is predominantly used for sparkling wine, but has come into its own as a table wine in the cooler parts of the country since the end of the 1980s.

Piquepoule noir. A minor red-grape variety from the Chateauneuf-du-Pape region of France, surviving as a few vines at Great Western.

Powdery: Similar to dusty, and almost inevitably deriving from prolonged old oak storage. Can be quite attractive.

Pressings: Wine recovered from pressing the skins, stalks and pips after fermentation. It is higher in tannin and may be deeper coloured. Often backblended into free-run wine to add strength and colour.

Puncheon: An oak barrel usually between 450 and 500 litres in capacity.

Pungent: Refers to a very aromatic wine with a high level of volatiles.

Punt: Indentation at the base of a bottle originally introduced to strengthen it.

Purple-red: A red wine colour in which the purple hues dominate the red; usually a young wine colour, and desirable.

Racking: Drawing off or decanting clear must or wine after allowing the lees to settle.

Rancio: Distinctive developed wood character of an old dessert wine stemming from a degree of oxidation. Highly desirable.

Raw: A term used to describe a sharp and aggressive oak flavour, due either to poor, unseasoned oak or to wine which has been removed from new oak barrels too quickly.

Red-purple: Applies to wine in which the red hues are more dominant than the purple: usually the first stage of colour change.

Reductive: A term used to describe a wine which has been rigorously protected from oxygen, and in which the fruit aroma may well be suppressed.

Residual sugar: Unfermented grape sugar remaining in white wine in the form of glucose and fructose. Can be tasted at levels in excess of five grams per litre. Many so-called dry rhine rieslings have six to seven grams per litre of residual sugar.

Riesling: In its native Germany is the most highly regarded white grape. Grown extensively around the world; known as white riesling or Johannisberg riesling in California and by a host of names in other countries. While it has fallen somewhat from public favour in Australia, it remains an important high-quality white grape. The widespread advent of botrytis has meant that both dry and very sweet wines of excellent quality can be made from it. While usually drunk young, the best rieslings can age for 15 or 20 years with surprising grace.

Rkatitseli: A Russian white grape propagated chiefly in the Griffith/Riverina.

Robust: Usually applied to a young red wine which needs further time in bottle.

Rootstock: The type of vine root onto which a scion or bearing grape vine is grafted. The scion, and not the rootstock, determines the grape type.

Rough: Astringent, coarse tannin taste in red wines indicating lack of balance and maturity.

Round: A well-balanced, smooth wine showing good fruit characters.

Roussanne: A white grape grown in the Rhône Valley and usually blended with marsanne. Also a minor component of some (red) Chateauneuf-du-Pape wines. Experimental plantings at Yeringberg in Yarra Valley.

Rubbery: The most common manifestation of hydrogen sulphide in the form of mercaptan.

Rubired: An American-bred red hybrid producing wines of startlingly intense colour and very useful for blending in small quantities for this purpose. Propagated on a limited scale in Australia.

Ruby cabernet: Another red hybrid bred by Professor Olmo at the University of California. Grown on a very limited scale in Australia.

Rulander: German synonym for pinot gris.

Sappy; sappiness: A touch of herbaceous or stalky character often found in young wines, particularly pinot noir, and usually a sign of potential quality.

Scented: A wine having a highly aromatic smell, usually associated with flowers or fruits.

Semillon: The major white grape of Bordeaux and the second most widely grown in the whole of France. Outside of France it is propagated chiefly in the southern hemisphere. Has been confused with chenin blanc in Western Australia and crouchen in South Australia; Barnawartha pinot of north-eastern Victoria is semillon. The classic white grape of the Hunter Valley: produces wines which are extremely long-lived and often need 10 years or more to reach their peak. Now also matured in new oak to produce a different style, and increasingly used for the production of sauternes-style wines in South Australia.

Sercial: Incorrect name for ondenc.

Shepherds riesling: An incorrect (and no longer used) name for semillon.

Shiraz: A red grape coming from the Hermitage area of the Rhône Valley, the origins of which are obscure and hotly debated. Frequently called hermitage in Australia (particularly in New South Wales and Victoria). For long the mainstay of the Australian red-wine industry, and still the most widely propagated red grape. The fact it can produce wines of the very highest quality was partially forgotten for a time, but no longer; a very versatile variety which can do well in all climates and soil types. Also useful for blending with cabernet sauvignon. Produces wines that richly repay cellaring, and is used solely in the production of Penfolds Grange, Australia's greatest and longest-lived red wine.

Silvaner; sylvaner: A vigorous high-yielding white grape extensively grown in Germany, producing rather neutral-flavoured wines, and even less distinguished wine in Australia.

Smooth: Agreeable and harmonious; opposite of astringent, harsh or rough.

Soft: Wine with a pleasing finish, neither hard nor aggressive. May indicate fairly low acid levels, but not necessarily so.

Solid: Unrelated to solids (see below); used in relation to aroma or flavour that is full or ample, but which possibly lacks subtlety.

Solids: Literally, suspended particles of skin and flesh in grape juice; when not removed from white grape juice prior to fermentation (by cold settling or filtration) may cause the finished wine to have a harsh, hard aroma, flavour and/or structure.

Sorbate: A chemical used to control oxidation but which imparts an unpleasant aroma and flavour.

Sour: Excessively acid, a character usually manifesting itself on the back of the palate.

Souzão: A minor red grape grown in the Douro Valley of Portugal.

Sparge: To saturate.

Spätlese: A German term for naturally sweet late-harvested wines, but appreciably less sweet than auslese.

Spice: A term used to denote any one of the numerous spice flavours which can occur in wines, deriving either from oak or from the grape itself. Most spicy characters are very pleasant and add to complexity. The actual spectrum is as broad as the name suggests, running from nutmeg to black pepper.

Spritz; spritzig: A German term indicating the presence of some carbon dioxide bubbles in the wine, frequently encountered in Australian white wine and occasionally in reds. Often an unintended consequence of protecting the wine from oxidation during storage and/or bottling. Can be felt as a slight prickle on the tongue.

Stabilisation: The chilling of a white wine to near-freezing point to precipitate tartaric crystals.

Stalky: Bitter character deriving from grape stalks, mainly appearing in red wines and indicative of poor winemaking.

Steen; stein: Incorrect names for chenin blanc used in South Africa.

Straw: Refers either to colour (self-explanatory) or to taste; in the latter context usually denotes a degree of oxidation.

Structure: An all-encompassing term covering all aspects of a wine other than its primary flavours, and includes alcohol, body, weight, tannin and acid, even though some of these also manifest themselves as flavours.

Stylish: A somewhat imprecise and subjective term to denote a wine which attractively conforms to varietal or generic style.

Sulphide; sulphidic: The generic term given to hydrogen sulphide and mercaptans.

Sulphur dioxide (SO$_2$): An antioxidant preservative used in virtually every wine — red, white or sparkling. In excessive quantities it imparts a disagreeable odour and may artificially retard the development of the wine. Dissipates with age.

Sultana: A white grape which originated in Asia Minor or the Middle East, and which is principally used both in Australia and elsewhere as a table grape. In California, where it is known as Thompson's seedless, it is grown on a very large scale and significant quantities are used for white-wine-making. When used for white-wine-making it produces a very neutral wine with quite good acidity.

Supple: A lively, yet round and satisfying wine.

Sweaty saddle: A description most frequently accorded to aged Hunter Valley reds, probably indicating the presence of some mercaptan, but curiously a term of commendation more than condemnation.

Sylvaner: See **Silvaner**.

Synonym: An alternative, though not officially preferred, grape variety name.

Syrah: Synonym for shiraz.

Tannin: A complex organic constituent of wine deriving chiefly from grape pips and stalks, and occurring in greater quantities in reds than in whites. Plays an important part in the self-clearing of young wines after fermentation, and thereafter in the period of maturation the wine requires: a full-bodied red, high in tannin, requires a longer period than does a lighter-bodied wine. Easily perceived in the taste of the wine by the slightly mouth-puckering, drying, furry sensation, particularly on the side of the tongue and on the gums. Some red-winemakers add powdered tannin to wine to increase the tannin level artificially.

Tarrango: A red hybrid grape bred by the CSIRO. Chiefly used in the production of nouveau-style reds by Brown Bros and others. Has considerable promise, but the wines made from it should not be cellared under any circumstances.

Tart: A wine with excess acid.

Tartaric acid: The principal naturally occurring acid in grapes, and added in powdered form to the vast majority of Australian white and red wines to compensate for the usually naturally deficient acid levels in ripe grapes.

Tartrate crystals: A natural deposit formed primarily of tartaric acid, but containing small quantities of other salts; harmless and largely tasteless.

Tawny:

(i)   The colour of an old red wine.

(ii) A wood-matured port.

Tempranillo: The most highly regarded of the red-grape varieties grown in Spain's Rioja, and known as valdepenas in California. A small planting by that name in the Upper Hunter Valley is presumably tempranillo. The wine matures extremely quickly.

Terret noir: A grape grown in the Languedoc area of France, appearing in three colour combinations — white, grey and black. A small planting of the latter type exists in the Barossa Valley.

Thick: Denotes an excessively heavy, and probably jammy, wine.

Thin: Lacking in body, almost watery and probably excessively acid.

Thompson's seedless: American synonym for sultana.

Tinta amarella: A red grape widely grown in the Douro Valley of Portugal and used in vintage port. There are small plantings in South Australia, where the variety is known as portugal. It has from time to time been confused with malbec.

Tinta cão: A red grape grown in the Douro Valley in Portugal and important in the making of vintage port. Only experimental plantings in Australia.

Toast; toasty: Literally the smell of fresh toast, occurring almost exclusively in white wines, and usually developing with bottle-age. Applies particularly to Hunter Valley semillon, but curiously, also to many rieslings.

Tobacco: Literally, the smell of tobacco.

Tokai friulano: A white grape closely related to sauvignon blanc and grown extensively in the Friuli-Venezia-Giulia region of north Italy. Grown on a large scale in Argentina where it is called sauvignon. Isolated vines exist in Mudgee, the Goulburn Valley and Great Western, sometimes in surprisingly large numbers. The wine has a definite bouquet and a slight bitterness, as its sauvignon blanc heritage would suggest.

Tokay: See **Muscadelle**.

Touriga: The most important red grape in the Douro Valley in Portugal, used extensively in vintage port. Small plantings have been grown for many years around Corowa, and there have been small recent plantings on the floor of the Barossa Valley. It is used to make high-quality vintage port, and a modest increase in plantings can be expected.

Traminer: An ancient white-grape variety derived from the primitive wild grapes of Europe. The main European plantings are in Alsace and Germany, and also northern Italy. Produces a highly aromatic wine which can quickly become overbearing and overblown. Contrary to public belief, there is no viticultural or other distinction between traminer and gewurztraminer, although the latter is supposedly more spicy in aroma and taste. By and large best drunk while fresh and young.

Trebbiano: The leading white grape of Italy, and now dominant in the Cognac region of France where it is known as St Emilion, although the official French name is ugni blanc. It is known by both these names in Australia and also (incorrectly) as white shiraz or white hermitage. It is grown in virtually all Australian wine regions, bearing well to produce a neutral and rather hard table wine and an excellent distillation base for brandy.

Trockenbeerenauslese: A German term for ultra-sweet white table wine made from hand-selected and picked berries, although in Australia there are no legal limits to its use.

Ugni blanc: French synonym for trebbiano.

Ullage: The air space present in a bottle of wine between the cork and the surface of the wine. In old wines it is a fairly reliable indication of likely quality: the greater the ullage, the more suspect the wine.

Valdepenas: Californian synonym for tempranillo.

Vanilla; vanillin: A sweet aroma usually derived from American oak, but also occurring in old bottle-developed white wines.

Varietal:
 (i) Character of wine derived from the grape.
 (ii) Generic term for wines made from a single or dominant variety and identified by reference to that variety.

Vat: A container in which wine is fermented, made of stainless steel, concrete or oak.

Vegetative: Normally indicates a rather dank, vegetable-like aroma, sometimes reminiscent of cabbage, and seldom desirable.

Velvety: The softly rich and smooth feel of an aged wine which has retained strong fruit flavour.

Veraison: The point at which the grapes start to change colour from green to red in the case of red grapes and from green to translucent green/yellow in the case of white grapes. A critical stage in the evolution of the vintage.

Verdelho: A white grape from Portugal, grown on the island of Madeira where it is used to make fortified wine, and in small quantities in the Douro Valley. The small Australian plantings are divided between Western Australia, South Australia and New South Wales. Produces a very distinctive, full-bodied table wine, and can also be used to make fortified wine. The table wines age well.

Vertical tasting: A tasting of different vintages of wine, usually from a single producer, but also possibly from a single variety or single district (involving different producers).

Vinification: The process of making wine.

Vinosity; vinous: A term relating to the strength of the grape character in a wine (though not necessarily the varietal character) and linked to the alcoholic strength of the wine. Denotes a desirable characteristic.

Viognier: A white grape grown chiefly at the northern end of the Rhône Valley to produce distinctive and highly-flavoured although relatively quick-maturing wine. Experimental plantings in Australia show some promise.

***Vitis aestivalis* and *Vitis labrusca*:** Species of vine native to North America with natural resistance to phylloxera and used as rootstocks in Europe and elsewhere.

***Vitis vinifera*:** The species of vine responsible for virtually all the wines of the world.

Volatile: A wine spoiled by an excess of acetic acid.

Volatile acid: A group of acids comprising acetic, carbonic, butyric, propionic and formic.

Volatility: Relating to the release of acetic acid and other esters, and which may be present to excess in a faulty wine.

Weight: Normally a measure of the strength of the wine in terms of alcohol and possibly tannin.

White frontignac: Synonym for muscat à petite grains.

White hermitage: Incorrect name for trebbiano.

White shiraz: Invalid name for trebbiano.

Yeast: Single-cell organism responsible for the fermentation of sugar into alcohol.

Yeasty: A smell or aroma deriving from the action of the yeast used to ferment the wine; except in the case of sparkling wine, should not be discernible to any degree.

Yellow-green: A white wine colour in which the yellow hues are more dominant than the green.

Zest; zesty: Used in relation to a wine which is very fresh and pleasantly lively and acidic.

Zinfandel: A grape variety grown chiefly in California, but may be related to the widely propagated primitivo variety of Italy. Grown in small quantities in Australia, chiefly in Western Australia and South Australia. Can produce a wine deep in colour and rich in soft, spicy flavour; it has an intermediate life span.

WINE

PURCHASED

Location	Opening Stock	Used	Date	TASTING NOTES/COMMENTS

index

more titles by james halliday
from harpercollins*publishers*

ISBN 0 207 19075 5

James Halliday's Australian and New Zealand Wine Companion 1998

n the *Wine Companion 1998*, James Halliday assesses the best currently available wines from Australian and New Zealand vineyards.

Each winery entry includes James Halliday's rating, the winery's address, phone/fax numbers and opening hours and its product range, and a concise summary of the winery and its wines. Each wine entry includes James Halliday's rating, the wine's price, background to its production, cellaring advice, best vintages, suggestions for compatible food choices and tasting notes on a current vintage. The easy-to-use alphabetical arrangement means you can find a winery, wine, or both, in an instant.

James Halliday's Australian and New Zealand Interactive Wine Companion

the new interactive CD-ROM for PC and Mac features James Halliday's detailed assessments of more than 1350 wines and 925 wineries; vertical tasting notes of over 90 classic wines, many going back 40 or 50 years; a step-by-step guide to tasting wine; interactive wine regions maps; and 'Ask James' — a video interview with the author. The versatile database allows you to set up records and tasting notes for your own wine cellar, and to compare your notes with those of the expert. With search and print facilities throughout, the *Interactive Wine Companion* is the perfect addition to every wine lover's collection.

ISBN 0 7322 5520 1

Wine Atlas of Australia and New Zealand

New revised edition

due out late 1998, this new edition offers all the detail and research of the previous edition and more. Including maps of Australia's new wine regions, profiles on Australia and New Zealand's top winemakers and wineries and stunning photographs by Oliver Strewe, the *Wine Atlas of Australia and New Zealand* is an indispensable reference tool.

ISBN 0 7322 64480

ISBN 0 7322 5789 1

Classic Wines of Australia

this unique book provides a comprehensive insight into the greatest wines made in Australia over the past 50 or more years. James Halliday's notes on vertical tastings of these wines cover all the most famous names; equally absorbing are the notes for the classics of tomorrow, wines known only to a chosen few. A brief introductory background is given to each of the 82 wines chosen, and tastings range far and wide across sparkling wines, white table wines — both dry and sweet — dry reds and fortified wines.

Some readers will already have cellars that include a number of these wines. Hopefully others will be inspired to start collecting wines and experiencing first hand the magical transformation of a vibrant young wine into a seriously graceful old wine.